THE SPIRITUAL JOURNEY

TOWARD A HEALED

MARRIAGE

"Have faith in God." Jesus answered. "I tell you the truth, if anyone says to this mountain, 'Go, throw yourself into the sea,' and does not doubt in his heart but believes that what he says will happen, it will be done for him."

Mark 11:22-23

By Charlyne Steinkamp

THE SPIRITUAL JOURNEY
TOWARD A HEALED MARRIAGE

ISBN 978-1-892230-16-4

by Charlyne A. Steinkamp

Rejoice Ministries, Inc.
Post Office Box 11242
Pompano Beach, Florida 33060
(954) 941-6508

www.rejoiceministries.org

Printed in the United States of America

ACKNOWLEDGMENTS

The words "Thank You" seem so inadequate when you have special people help you print and publish a book. When you write a book, you have this inner desire to write down what you want to share from your heart. Then you need help doing the typing, the retyping, the editing, the proofing, and the graphics for the cover. Someone must spend hours checking the Scriptures.

Every person working on this manuscript volunteered their time and talents. I pray that the Lord will bless each of them in a very special way.

Bob and I are very blessed knowing some fantastic people with super skills. Denise Ramsay helped with typing the manuscript and worked with all the Scriptures. Dennis Wingfield, Lorrie Meininger and Kathie C. Johnson, a Professor at Liberty University each shared their time and expertise proofing the manuscript. Beatriz Montalvo and Beverly Dillon-Petruschke, two special standers, also helped with the manuscript. Thank you all so very much!

I had many people looking for a picture that I had in my mind for the book's cover. My daughter, Lori's mother-in-law, and my friend, Linda Lassen had gone to California to Yosemite National Park. She gave me all her pictures and I found just the right one that spoke to my heart and went with the scripture on the cover of the book. God is so faithful! He puts all the pieces of the puzzle together in His perfect timing. Thank you Linda for going to California on vacation!

You can have a picture, but unless you have the right person be able to put it together and make it come alive in color, it is only a photograph. Don W. Hardin from Image House Designs, Inc. used his talents and expertise to make the beautiful cover for our book. This is the third book cover that

Don has done for us.

Last year at this time, I did not believe this book would ever be finished and printed. I personally had to go on my own *Spiritual Journey* with my Lord. I found out seventeen years ago, before you can share a testimony, you have to go through a trial.

This past year I had to apply all the principles and precepts I have shared in this book to my own personal life. Thank you Lord, your Word never fails! God is faithful, He will never you leave you and He will guide you every step of the way. Thank you Lord, for allowing this book to be printed. May it bring glory and honor to You alone!

Charlyne Steinkamp

DEDICATION

I want to dedicate this book to the Prayer Warriors around the world who believe in the power of prayer. We have Prayer Warriors from many countries, praying and believing for God's special touch on marriages, families, children, grandchildren and all the trials and circumstances that come when the enemy tries to kill, steal and destroy marriages and families.

Prayer Warriors are special people as they do not look at the circumstances, but keep their eyes on their awesome mighty Lord God who created the earth, who can part the Red Sea and who can move mountains, if we would only believe.

We have *Pray 24* on our Internet site, where people can sign up to pray 15 minute daily for hurting families around the world. Each person is sacrificing their time to stand for the sanctity and the holiness of marriage. God created marriage and He hates divorce. Should we be any different? May we continue to pray in agreement for a mighty revival, an outpouring of the Holy Spirit to touch, restore, rebuild and reconcile all couples, families and children around the world. Sin has destroyed families, but God sent His Son as a sacrifice for all sinners, including our loved ones. May we never give up on any one person. God does heal and restore sinners. God does answer prayers every day!

Rejoice Marriage Ministries would probably not be in existence today if it were not for all the Prayers Warriors that have prayed for Bob and me, and this ministry since its birth.

No words can ever say "Thank You" enough. You are very special people! May the Lord bless you abundantly!

God bless you,
Charlyne

INDEX

FOREWORD

We prodigals do not forget what we know when we run from God. We may attempt to put His truths aside, but they keep darting out right in front of us, at the most unexpected times, while we travel on a dead end road, searching for a place called Happiness. That destination will continue to escape us until we turn right. Please start the *Spiritual Journey* my wife is mapping out for you. Your mate's path can best be changed by first changing your own path.

Yes, there is a way home. That journey is mapped out in God's Word, the Holy Bible, and our Navigator, who will never fail us, is our Lord Jesus Christ. May God bless us as we travel His way.

Bob Steinkamp

WHEN YOUR SPOUSE WALKS OUT!!

The one you love, that one who stood and made a covenant with you to, *"love, honor and cherish, 'til death do us part"* has left. Your visions of a happy family and of a future together have been shattered. Two families each minute are being destroyed by divorce. This epidemic is reaching once-happy homes, leaving behind brokenhearted spouses and children.

Everyone seems to offer advice, but no one has a solution. Where do you turn? Who will help you? What do you do? Yes, you will survive. Yes, there is help available.

In 1985, my husband, Bob, became the Prodigal Son of our family, as he left his home, wife and three children, in an attempt to start all over again with someone new.

The hurt that followed cannot be described. Only one who's been there knows the emotions that follow separation. We experience, fear, rejection, anger, hopelessness, and yes, even a bit of hope.

That glimmer of hope became the foundation of my stand for a restored marriage. That stand for marriage restoration was fulfilled two years after our divorce was final. That day we stood in our pastor's office and were, once again, pronounced man and wife.

That hope for marriage restoration did not belong to our family alone. It is available for you. Yes, divorces do take place, but even more important, families are also being restored. Don't bury your marriage when there's still life in it. Granted, your relationship may need some resuscitation, as did ours a few years ago, but it can be healthy again.

DON'T LOOK AT CIRCUMSTANCES - Your circumstances may, as did mine, look impossible. There was another person involved. My husband wanted out. He was unwilling to work on our marriage. He had declared clearly, by word and deed, how little our family meant to him. Looking at circumstances would cause both you and I to give up. Look to the realistic hope of a restored marriage, not to that mountain of circumstances.

"ZIP THE LIPS" - Although it's a bit harsh, scores have found that to be good advice. Many a spouse have found the way back home made difficult by words strewn to others by a hurting and abandoned mate. Find one friend, of the same sex, one who will

GOING ON A *SPIRITUAL JOURNEY!*

Do you have marriage problems? Are you separated or divorced? Bob and I had marriage problems seventeen years ago, to the extent that we got divorced. I am writing this book to help people around the world to believe in the power of God and the power of prayer. My prayer is that every word I write show you that nothing is too hard for your Lord God to fix. Yes, I said **"nothing"** is too hard for the Creator, the Counselor and the Great Physician who can touch and change your heart and then go touch and work on your spouse's heart.

God created marriage and hates divorce. Our nation and churches are compromising God's standard by winking at the consequences of divorce to our families, to our children, to our loved ones and to our churches. The church is not able to be the "Critical Care Unit" for the wounded and broken hearts as divorce is rampart within the church. We are going to discuss throughout this book the reasons why spouses are leaving home and what you and I can do about separation and divorce destroying our homes and loved ones.

The Lord God said, "It is not good for the man to be alone. I will make a helper suitable for him"...Then the Lord God made a woman from the rib he had taken out of the man, and he brought her to the man...For this reason a man will leave his father and mother and be united to his wife, and they will become one flesh.

Genesis 2:18,22,24

...So guard yourself in your spirit, and do not break faith with the wife of your youth. "I hate divorce," says the Lord God of Israel.

Malachi 2:15-16

I would like to take you on a *Spiritual Journey* with your Lord. You may be starting a new walk with the Lord or you maybe doing a self-examination of where you are spiritually and where you need to be with your Lord God. Let's get started by seeking the Lord and putting His Words into practice for all your problems!

"Ah, Sovereign Lord, you have made the heavens and the earth by your great power and outstretched arm. Nothing is too hard for you....I am the Lord, the God of all mankind. Is anything too hard for me?"

Jeremiah 32:17,27

Your spouse may have just told you they are leaving and that they do not love you. In fact, they may say they do not think they really ever loved you. Your spouse is determined to terminate your marriage regardless of your pleas. They say they need time to think and they are moving out of the house to do this. Some spouses say that and start the process of leaving, but may stay at home. If they do, ask the Lord to show you how to love them unconditionally. The Lord can still touch their heart. Once a person starts speaking separation and divorce, know that the enemy is tempting them to fall into sin. You need to become the prayer warrior for your family. You need to start immediately.

You do not know what to do or where to go. You may be very active in a church, some of you are wives of pastors or your spouse may be in a ministry. The enemy is no respecter of persons. Your home has just been attacked and bombed like the Twin Towers in New York City. You need to run to the Lord for His safety, His wisdom and His knowledge. He will protect and guide you from now on. You are in shock, you are hurting, but your Lord God has ALL the answers! Seek the Lord to *change* you first to become the person that the He wants you to be. While the Lord is changing you, your spouse will start to notice that you are becoming different!

You may have known, deep in your heart, that there were problems in your marriage, but everyone has problems once in a while. You were giving your spouse time to start acting and feeling better. You were not sure if there were problems at work which were causing them some stress or pressure. Now your spouse blames you, possibly for all the problems. Some prodigal spouses take the blame completely and say it is not your fault, but there is nothing you can do to rebuild or restore your marriage. They want a divorce.

Your spouse has been on an emotional detour being tempted in their thought process to getting off the road of marriage. They have thought of every excuse as to why they need to separate and live a separate life. Reasoning does not work at all. The children? Your children can adjust. Your spouse is saying, "Fifty percent of all marriages have problems that end up in divorce. We are not any different! It will be better for each of us, including the children, they won't have to listen to our bickering, arguing, and fighting."

Usually at this point, most people will not reconsider. Some may agree to try to work with a counselor to try to save their marriage. The enemy, their friends and the world have brainwashed them that separation and divorce is NO BIG DEAL!

There is really little that you can do at this moment, except pray that the Holy Spirit will speak to their heart. It is not always the men that leave home, there are many women who leave their homes. Some of these women leave their children, some share them, and some keep them. Separation and divorce are very devastating to every member of the family.

We need to realize that as in New York City or Oklahoma City many years ago when the bomb suddenly went off it destroyed many lives and shocked many people.

Your separation and/or divorce will do likewise. You need to pull your emotions and feelings together and get on your knees seeking your Heavenly Father for a plan to get you through this tragedy in your marriage.

My prayer for you is:

....that the God of our Lord Jesus Christ, the glorious Father, may give you the Spirit of wisdom and revelation, so that you may know him better. I pray that out of his glorious riches he may strengthen you with power through his Spirit in your inner being, so that Christ may dwell in your hearts through faith.

Ephesians 1:17 & 3:16

...we have not stopped praying for you and asking God to fill you with the knowledge of his will through all spiritual wisdom and understanding.

Colossians 1:9

I know that many of you are in the very early stages of "standing" and praying for your marriage. The pain in your heart is unbearable. You have been rejected by the one you have given your life to, the one you love and care for; ONLY to be abused emotionally, verbally, and possibly physically. Some of you may already be separated or divorced. Still others have your spouse at home, or your spouse has come back home after being gone for a season, but has not repented or has not been cleaned up completely by the Lord! Only your Lord God can heal your wounded heart, regardless of your present circumstances.

The Lord is close to the brokenhearted and saves those who are crushed in spirit.

Psalm 34:18

The Spirit of the Sovereign Lord is on me, because the Lord has anointed me to preach good news to the poor. He has sent me to bind up the brokenhearted, to proclaim freedom for the captives and release from darkness for the prisoners, to proclaim the year of the Lord's favor and the day of vengeance of our God, to comfort all who mourn, and provide for those who grieve in Zion— to bestow on them a crown of beauty instead of ashes, the oil of gladness instead of mourning, and a garment of praise instead of a spirit of despair. They will be called oaks of righteousness, a planting of the Lord for the display of his splendor. They will rebuild the ancient ruins and restore the places long devastated; they will renew the ruined cities that have been devastated for generations.

Isaiah 61:1-4

Yes, there are many of you who have been standing for a season and are questioning, "Lord, is my spouse ever coming home?" If that is the case, may this become a *new Spiritual Journey* to give you a closer, more powerful insight of God's will for your life today! New manna for you everyday!

I want to share from my heart and guide you on a *Spiritual Journey* where your Lord God is waiting for you to call on Him. I hope you will seek Him with all your heart.

I will instruct you and teach you in the way you should go; I will counsel you and watch over you.

Psalm 32:8

Listen to my prayer, O God, do not ignore my plea; hear me and answer me. My thoughts trouble me and I am distraught at the voice of the enemy...But I call to God, and the Lord saves me. Evening, morning and noon I cry out in distress, and he hears my voice.

Psalm 55:1-3,16-17

Are you ready to start this *Spiritual Journey* by surrendering your ALL to the Lord? Are you ready to admit that you may have made a mess out of your life and marriage? Do you need His help to straighten it out? Are you willing to admit that you have lived your life so far "your way" and now you want to know His will for your life? Are you tired and weary? Have you become broken enough that you want to do it His way and only His way? Do not worry how you or the Lord can fix or mend your hopeless marriage. Admit you need God's help!

We wait in hope for the Lord; he is our help and our shield.
Psalm 33:20

Do you fear God? **We all need to fear God.** Let's pray that our prodigals and all our loved ones will fear God, to be obedient to His will, and His way.

Come, my children, listen to me; I will teach you the fear of the Lord.
Psalm 34:11

Start this new journey today by crying out to your Lord and Savior. Make a commitment to Him and to the one you love forever.

Dear children, let us not love with words or tongue but with actions and in truth.
I John 3:18

LORD, HELP ME!

Is this your heart's cry today? I hope so. I know each of you never thought you would be going through all that you are going through. You dreamed of having a marriage of love, babies, a new house, a new car, with financial security, goals and dreams of your future. Your wedding was beautiful and look at your wedding pictures! What happened?

"What am I suppose to do? My spouse wants to separate or divorce me! I never thought our problems would come to this point? I can not believe this is really happening. My heart is hurting so bad. I am so scared. Abba Father, Help me! Daddy, I want to get to know you! I hear people talk about You all the time, but I do not know You that way! Help me!"

O Lord, do not forsake me; be not far from me, O my God. Come quickly to help me, O Lord my Savior.
Psalm 38:21-22

I sought the Lord, and he answered me; he delivered me from all my fears....This poor man called, and the Lord heard him; he saved him out of all his troubles...The eyes of the Lord are on the righteous and his ears are attentive to their cry;...
Psalm 34:4,6,15

I hope this is your heart's deepest cry today. I was a Christian when Bob and I were having marriage problems. We went to Pastors and Counselors, but I did not have a deep personal relationship with my Lord as I do now. I did not read the Word or pray daily as I do now. Your Lord God is waiting for your cry for help. He will never leave or forsake you. He is right there with you!

He heals the brokenhearted and binds up their wounds.

Psalm 147:3

The angel of the Lord encamps around those who fear him, and he delivers them. Taste and see that the Lord is good; blessed is the man who takes refuge in him...but those who seek the Lord lack no good thing.

Psalm 34:7-8,10

I pray that out of your tragedy, your despair, your pain, your shame and the rejection that you are going through, you will meet your Abba, Father in a new way. Once you meet Him this way, you will never want to go back. Your Heavenly Father cares about you! He wants a personal relationship with you. He loves you right where you are today, with no conditions. He died for you alone.

Show me your ways, O Lord, teach me your paths; guide me in your truth and teach me, for you are God my Savior, and my hope is in you all day long.

Psalm 25:4-5

Teach me to do your will, for you are my God; may your good Spirit lead me on level ground.

Psalm 143:10

"I desire to do your will, O my God; your law is within my heart."

Psalm 40:8

The righteous cry out, and the Lord hears them; he delivers them from all their troubles. The Lord is close to the brokenhearted and saves those who are crushed in spirit. A righteous man may have many troubles, but the Lord delivers him from them all...The Lord redeems his servants; no one will be condemned who takes refuge in him.

Psalm 34:17-19,22

Most of our standers who have had this spiritual encounter or had this spiritual awakening say, "It was worth going through my circumstances to know my Lord this new way!" Many have come to know Jesus Christ as their Lord and Savior during this crisis. Where are you today? Allow the Holy Spirit to minister to you right now, where you are. Ask Him to forgive you of your sins. Ask Him to forgive you of your part of your marriage problems. Believe in the power of your Lord God, that He loves both you and your spouse so much, that He wants both of you to repent and turn to Him to heal, restore and rebuild your marriage on the solid rock of Jesus Christ.

Those whom I love I rebuke and discipline. So be earnest, and repent. Here I am! I stand at the door and knock. If anyone hears my voice and opens the door, I will come in and eat with him, and he with me.

Revelation 3:19-20

Peter replied, "Repent and be baptized, every one of you, in the name of Jesus Christ for the forgiveness of your sins. And you will receive the gift of the Holy Spirit. The promise is for you and your children and for all who are far off — for all whom the Lord our God will call.

Acts 2:38-39

I tell you that in the same way there will be more rejoicing in heaven over one sinner who repents than over ninety-nine righteous persons who do not need to repent.

Luke 15:7

Trust in the Lord with all your heart and lean not on your own understanding; in all your ways acknowledge him, and he will make your paths straight.

Proverbs 3:5-6

You may have never made that final commitment to accepting Jesus Christ as Savior and Lord. Today cry out to

Him, repenting and asking the Lord to come into your heart and life.

The first step in a healed, restored marriage is to have a personal relationship with Jesus Christ. Our Lord God and Creator is waiting to hear your prayer. Have you received Jesus Christ as Lord and Savior of your life? He will save you and be your Comforter and Counselor in the days ahead, regardless of your circumstances.

If we confess our sins, he is faithful and just and will forgive us our sins and purify us from all unrighteousness.
I John 1:9

You will find rest and joy in His arms. He wants to meet your every need. He wants to have a deep, intimate, personal relationship with you. You may have a head knowledge, but I want you to have a heart knowledge that will transform your life. You will never be the same. Praise the Lord!

A PRAYER FOR YOU TO PRAY

Dear Jesus, I believe that You died for me and that You rose again on the third day. I confess to You that I am a sinner and that I need Your love and forgiveness. Come into my life, forgive me of my sins, and give me eternal life. I confess to You now that You are my Lord and Savior. Thank You for my salvation. Lord, show me Your will and Your way for my marriage. Mold me and make me to be the mate I need to be for my spouse. Thank You in advance and by faith for rebuilding and restoring my marriage. *Amen.*

Believe in the Lord Jesus, and you will be saved--you and your household.
Acts 16:31

It will take time to get to know Him. Start with five or ten minutes a day, increasing your time. Ask the Lord to show you how to make time for Him, He is very creative. Remember, if you want to get to know someone you must spend time with them daily.

"Be still, and know that I am God;...."

Psalm 46:10

Read **Psalm 139.** God created you and knows your innermost being. Do not listen to what your spouse is saying about you right now. That is not Jesus talking. Their words try to justify their actions, to meet their own selfish needs, self-centerness and sinful nature. What does the Bible say about you? He created you and has a plan and a purpose for your life, even right now!

For you created my inmost being; you knit me together in my mother's womb. I praise you because I am fearfully and wonderfully made;....

Psalm 139:13-14

"For I know the plans I have for you," declares the Lord, "plans to prosper you and not to harm you, plans to give you hope and a future."

Jeremiah 29:11

Though I walk in the midst of trouble, you preserve my life; you stretch out your hand against the anger of my foes, with your right hand you save. The Lord will full his purpose for me; your love, O Lord, endures forever--do not abandon the works of your hands.

Psalm 138:7-8

Many of you say you are scared to be alone. Ask the Lord to deepen your relationship with Him. Your Lord God is with you all the time. Read **Psalm 91.**

I pray that out of his glorious riches he may strengthen you with power through his Spirit in your inner being, so that Christ may dwell in your hearts through faith. And I pray that you being rooted and established in love, may have power , together with all the saints, to grasp how wide and long and high and deep is the love of Christ.

Ephesians 3:16-18

"Because he loves me," says the Lord, "I will rescue him; I will protect him, for he acknowledges my name. He will call upon me, and I will answer him; I will be with him in trouble, I will deliver him and honor him."

Psalm 91:14-15

Begin today, spend time with Him. He is waiting for you to call Him today, "Abba, Father, here I am."

A PRAYER FOR YOU TO PRAY

Lord, here I am, Your child. I am hurting so badly, but I am seeking Your help. I pray that You will come alive to me in a way that I have never known You. Lord, help me to believe in You and Your power. Help me believe that You can restore, rebuild my marriage. Father, increase my faith in You as I read this book. Open my spiritual ears, take any blinders off my eyes and bind the enemy so that I can believe Your every Word as I read. *Amen.*

A BOBSERVATION

My wife lives exactly as she has shared. I could not "push her buttons" when we were reconciling 16 years ago, and I still can't find them to push today. She gives every worry and concern to the Lord, so that she can live consistently for Him. I pray that you can do likewise. That is the only way that you will make it through your problems.

Your life may seem as though you are being flung off of a tall, burning building named *Divorce Tower*. Far below you see the only one who can rescue you, but He is so distant. Call out to Him today, "Daddy, save me! Rescue me before I crash!" Your life can seem as though you are slowing down floating softly into the big, loving arms of a God who cares. After this marriage crisis has passed, God will still be holding you, protecting you, saving you, guiding you, and loving you. That is what Charlyne is encouraging you to do, and I say, *Amen!*

HELP I'M IN TROUBLE!

Are you needing help? What are you going to do with so many marriage problems and no answers? Where do you go for help? What are the right answers and who do you ask for guidance? Do you feel helpless? I did. When Bob was out in the pigpen of life, I not only faced problems, but I did not have a spouse to help me come up with the solutions.

Read **Psalm 56** for your devotion today. When you have problems or if fear is coming against you, praise the Lord. Praise the Lord for who He is, for His commands, for His scriptures and for His protection.

Be merciful to me, O God, for men hotly pursue me; all day long they press their attack...When I am afraid, I will trust in you. In God, whose word I praise, in God I trust; I will not be afraid. What can mortal man do to me?
Psalm 56:1,3-4

The Lord gave me Isaiah 54:17 when I was learning to pray for my husband and my children. I kept repeating it throughout the day when all the circumstances were coming against me. When I said it, I felt such a peace from God. I learned to stand and believe in the promises of God. I really did not understand the promises of the Bible at the beginning of my stand, but the Lord taught me the power of His Word.

"No weapon formed against you shall prosper."
Isaiah 54:17 NKJV

Have mercy on me, O God, have mercy on me, for in you my soul takes refuge. I will take refuge in the shadow of your wings until the disaster has passed. I cry out to God Most High, to God, who fulfills his purpose for me.
Psalm 57:1-2

Do you believe this? Do you believe in the power of the Lord? Your Lord God will become your Protector and Deliverer. Remind yourself everyday that God is on your side! The enemy has attacked your home and your spouse is blinded, deceived and brainwashed.

Regardless of any of the circumstances that are overwhelming you, know that God is in full control of your every step. He can shut the lion's mouth. He can keep the fire from burning you. He can defeat your enemies. He rescued people throughout the Bible and He is no respecter of persons. He will rescue you everyday of your life.

You are my hiding place; you will protect me from trouble and surround me with songs of deliverance.
Psalm 32:7

You are of God, little children, and have overcome them, because He who is in you is greater than he who is in the world.
I John 4:4 NKJV

Keep looking up to your Lord and not at all your circumstances. Trust Him. Believe in His Word and claim the promises that He has given you. He will never leave or forsake you or your family. He wants you to be the lighthouse for your family. Let your beacon shine through the clouds that now seem to surround you.

"Be strong and courageous. Do not be afraid or terrified because of them, for the Lord your God goes with you; he will never leave you nor forsake you."
Deuteronomy 31:6

When I am afraid, I will trust in you. In God, whose word I praise, in God I trust; I will not be afraid. What can mortal man do to me? All day long they twist my words; they are always plotting to harm me. They conspire, they lurk, they watch my steps, eager to take my life....Then my enemies will turn back when I call for help. By this I will know that God is for me. In God, whose word I praise, in the Lord, whose word I praise--in God I trust; I will not be afraid. What can man do to me?....For you have delivered me from death and my feet from stumbling, that I may walk before God in the light of life.

Psalm 56:3-6,9-11,13

"He said: "The Lord is my rock, my fortress and my deliverer; my God is my rock, in whom I take refuge, my shield and the horn of my salvation. He is my stronghold, my refuge and my savior--from violent men you save me. I call to the Lord, who is worthy of praise, and I am saved from my enemies....He reached down from on high and took hold of me; he drew me out of deep waters. He rescued me from my powerful enemy, from my foes, who were too strong for me. They confronted me in the day of my disaster, but the Lord was my support. He brought me out into a spacious place; he rescued me because he delighted in me".

2 Samuel 22:2-4,17-20

LORD, WHY DID THIS HAPPEN?

Praise be to the God and Father of our Lord Jesus Christ, the Father of compassion and the God of all comfort, who comforts us in all our troubles, so that we can comfort those in any trouble with the comfort we ourselves have received from God.

2 Corinthians 1:3-4

Many of you may never know the exact reason "why" your spouse left, but God will show you His way. Many things happened to Bob and me in our marriage and divorce, so that we can share the love, the faithfulness and the power of our Lord Jesus Christ with you. If you do not have a testimony of triumph and victory now in your trials, wait on the Lord. In the future, you will be able to share the power of your Lord God.

God is all you need when you are in trouble. He will meet your every need. Surrender your all to Him. Cry out to Him.

God wants to teach each of us the power of prayer and the *power* in our daily relationship with Him. Are you learning? I hope so. I can truly say it was a blessing from God when He allowed me to go to the bottom by trying to fix my marriage "my way and by myself." I made a mess of my marriage and divorce. I then cried out to Him looking up to Him for His divine intervention. His way is the ONLY way that will last!

"...The wall of Jerusalem is broken down, and its gates have been burned with fire." When I heard these things, I sat down and wept. For some days I mourned and fasted and prayed before the God of heaven. Then I said: "O Lord, God of heaven, the great and awesome God, who keeps his covenant of love with those who love him and obey his commands, let your ear be attentive and your eyes open to hear the prayer

-17-

your servant is praying before you day and night for your servants, the people of Israel....but if you return to me and obey my commands, then even if your exiled people are at the farthest horizon, I will gather them from there and bring them to the place I have chosen as a dwelling for my Name."

Nehemiah 1:3-6,9

"...But this happened that we might not rely on ourselves but on God, who raises the dead. He has delivered us from such a deadly peril, and he will deliver us. On him we have set our hope that he will continue to deliver us."

2 Corinthians 1:9-10

Yes, you and I may be listed as strange or peculiar people at our church or in our Sunday School class. Many people would say, "You have such faith! I wish I had that much faith!" They can have that same faith for so many other things, if only they would understand the Word of God and what faith really means.

"Being confident of this, that he who began a good work in you will carry it on to completion until the day of Christ Jesus."

Philippians 1:6

Bob and I pray daily that your marriage will be restored. We pray that your spouse will repent and turn from their evil ways. We pray that each and every prodigal will be obedient and sensitive to the Holy Spirit's wooing.

We pray that in a few day, a few months, or in God's timing each of you will be able to say:

...Yes, and I will continue to rejoice, for I know that through your prayers and the help given by the Spirit of Jesus Christ, what has happened to me will turn out for my deliverance.

Philippians 1:18-19

Praise the Lord for His faithfulness for He will deliver each of us and our loved ones from the enemy! He paid the price on the cross of Calvary by shedding His blood for you and me. There is power in the blood and in the name of **JESUS!**

I consider that our present sufferings are not worth comparing with the glory that will be revealed in us....And we know that in all things God works for the good of those who love him who have been called according to his purpose.

Romans 8:18,28

A PRAYER FOR YOU TO PRAY

Lord, I do not understand why these marriage problems have happened to me and our family. I wanted our family to be the godly, perfect family in our church and neighborhood. Lord, teach me what I need to do. Help me never to give up on my spouse that I love so much, who is hurting me and so many others right now. Lord, come and be my spouse and the other parent in our home. Guide my every step. I do not understand why this has happened, but I am believing You to turn all this to good in the future. In Jesus's Name. *Amen.*

LISTEN AND OBEY!

I would like to challenge each of you to **LISTEN** for the Lord's voice. Yes, **LISTEN** for the Lord to speak to YOU! When I started praying for Bob, I did not know or believe that I could hear God's voice. Now I ask people each day, "Has the Lord spoken to you?" If not, seek Him, and then listen to His still small voice. Listening is an important spiritual skill that you need to develop.

"Go near and listen to all that the Lord our God says. Then tell us whatever the Lord our God tells you. We will listen and obey. . . . Oh, that their hearts would be inclined to fear me and keep all my commands always so that it might go well with them and their children forever!"
Deuteronomy 5:27,29

"Then you will call upon me and come and pray to me, and I will listen to you. You will seek me and find me when you seek me with all your heart."
Jeremiah 29:12-13

Let the wise listen and add to their learning, and let the discerning get guidance.
Proverbs 1:5

"I do not know what to do. I do not know where to live. I do not know how I am going to pay all the bills. I do not know whether to file for divorce since my spouse is unfaithful. My pastor and counselor are recommending 'tough love,' what should I do? I am angry, I am hurt and I am scared about my future." Are those your thoughts and fears? Bob and I could write 25 more statements that each of you say or write to us, but I want to encourage you regardless of the questions in your life--

GO TO THE LORD AND ASK HIM WHAT TO DO! HE WILL SPEAK TO YOU, GUIDE YOU, PROVIDE FOR YOU AND DIRECT YOUR EVERY STEP!

" '...Speak, Lord, for your servant is listening.' "

I Samuel 3:9

Read **I Samuel Chapter 3**. Listening to the Lord does take time. Take extra time this week to be quiet from the noise and activity of your busy life. Listen humbly and quietly for his guidance.

Every time you pray and do devotions ask the Lord to speak to you. If your devotions especially speak to your heart or seem to leap off the page, God is speaking to you. At the end of your prayer time, ask the Lord if He wants to speak to your heart anymore. Then just sit there and wait for the Lord to speak to you. Learn to listen to His soft small voice, the Holy Spirit.

"My sheep listen to my voice; I know them, and they follow me."

John 10:27

Whether you turn to the right or to the left, your ears will hear a voice behind you, saying, "This is the way; walk in it."

Isaiah 30:21

The Lord will speak to you. Do not ask us how it will happen, just be available and say to the Lord as Moses said in **Exodus Chapter 3:4,** *"Here I am."* We have heard many stories that are awesome about God speaking to His children. He does it different ways at different times. So be patient, especially if you are a young Christian. Spiritual listening involves your heart, your mind, your spiritual eyes and your spiritual ears. God will speak, but He also wants us to obey Him after He speaks.

Our God speaks to his children to pray and "stand" for their marriage before they even know what "standing" is. God speaks to prodigals daily telling them to be obedient to His will and His way. Today know for certain that God tells prodigals daily to **GO HOME, BUT THEY ARE BEING DISOBEDIENT!** They do not **FEAR** God.

Learn to **LISTEN** to Your Lord. As you listen to what God's Word say, may you allow your Bible study time to affect your behavior, your attitudes and your actions. Let's pray that each child of God and each prodigal will be obedient to God's commands daily! **LISTEN AND THEN OBEY GOD!**

A SPECIAL PRAYER FOR YOU

Lord, I pray that You will speak to this special child in a mighty way. Open their spiritual eyes and ears to see things that they have never seen or heard before. Thank You for allowing me to teach Your Word and Your power to this precious child of Yours. May they hunger for Your Word and deepen their walk and relationship with You daily. *Amen.*

Now to him who is able to do immeasurably more than all we ask or imagine, according to his power that is at work within us.

Ephesians 3:20

LORD HEAR MY CRY!

Out of the depths I cry to you, O Lord; O Lord, hear my voice. Let your ears be attentive to my cry for mercy.

Psalm 130:1-2

Is this your cry today? I know that He knows how you hurt inside, and He knows all your fears and anxieties from A to Z. I pray that today you will believe me and know for certain that God loves you and will guide your every footstep. He is there with you all the time.

"...I will never leave you nor forsake you."

Joshua 1:5

The eyes of the Lord are on the righteous and his ears are attentive to their cry;....The righteous cry out, and the Lord hears them; he delivers them from all their troubles.

Psalm 34:15,17

"...We do not know what to do, but our eyes are upon you."

2 Chronicles 20:12

May **Jeremiah 33:3** come alive to you today. He is waiting for you to cry out to Him in your brokenness and He will begin the healing process for you and your family. Cry out to your Heavenly, Abba Father and then listen for what He wants to show and tell you today. **He is the only one who can really change anything in your life forever**!

'Call to me and I will answer you and tell you great and unsearchable things you do not know.'

Jeremiah 33:3

He will tell you things that you do not know and can never imagine. If you do not know what to do, spend time with Him.

Listen to His soft voice. Read and study His Word. He has a plan and a purpose for you and your family, even through this crisis of marriage problems, separation or divorce. Memorize and always remember one of my favorite scriptures.

"For I know the plans I have for you," declares the Lord, "plans to prosper you and not to harm you, plans to give you hope and a future. Then you will call upon me and come and pray to me, and I will listen to you. You will seek me and find me when you seek me with all your heart".
                                                    Jeremiah 29:11-13

And we know that in all things God works for the good of those who love him, who have been called according to his purpose...If God is for us, who can be against us?...No, in all these things we are more than conquerors through him who loved us.
                                                    Romans 8:28,31,37

All of you have been hurt, wounded and abandoned by someone that you deeply love. Because of the pain, hurt and rejection you have been going through, the enemy may use anger, bitterness and hatred to come into your own life. Beware of the enemy's tricks. Know who the enemy is. It is not your spouse - they have been deceived and taken captive by the enemy.

For our struggle is not against flesh and blood, but against the rulers, against the authorities, against the powers of this dark world and against the spiritual forces of evil in the heavenly realms.
                                                    Ephesians 6:12

Do you know for certain that there really is a God? Do you know that He really answers prayers, especially your prayers? Cry out to Him. Do not wait another day, because He is waiting to meet you and to show you His wonderful love and power!

"He will call upon me, and I will answer him; I will be with him in trouble, I will deliver him and honor him."

Psalm 91:15

Many of you are going through of trials and circumstances that no one else knows about. The enemy is out to destroy you and your family. Some of you are experiencing spiritual, emotional and physical stress, children becoming disobedient, or financial pressures and you do not see a way out.

Only God can rescue you. Cry out to Him. Be like Moses, when the only hope for him and his people was to "sell out, totally surrender and yield their all to Him." That is when you will see the hand of God start moving in your life.

Moses answered the people, "Do not be afraid. Stand firm and you will see the deliverance the Lord will bring you today...The Lord will fight for you; you need only to be still."

Exodus 14:13-14

May I challenge you to seek the Lord. Ask Him your questions. Listen to Him for your answers. Do not take surveys from all your family and friends. They will not be giving you God's plan or assignment for your life. You will find your Lord God's plan when you cry out to Him with all your heart! He is waiting for you!

A PRAYER FOR YOU TO PRAY

Lord, hear my cry to show me Your will and Your way in my life. I never thought I would be facing these circumstances. Please help me! Forgive me of my weaknesses, my doubts and my fears. Lord, I want to follow You, but many times I do not even know if You are with me. Lord, reveal Yourself to me in a new and supernatural way that I have never known before. I know You speak to Your sheep, so speak loudly and clearly so that I know what to do and **be obedient to do Your will.** Thank You for the Holy Spirit and the power You have left me for times like this. I love and praise Your Holy Name. *Amen.*

A BOBSERVATION

If you ask the same question enough times, someone will give you the wrong answer that you want to hear. Every day we receive mail that reports, "My friend/Pastor/parents/whomever said...."

Our question to that individual is, "Why were you even asking them? What does God say?" That alone must be your final answer. Do not depend on the audience survey, for they may be wrong. Cry out to God, as Charlyne suggests today, and then wait and listen for His answer.

I DO NOT KNOW WHAT TO DO!

"Lord, there are so many people who want to do Your will, may You show them what You would have them do. Speak clearly and loudly so they know You are speaking to them. In Jesus name, *Amen.*"

"...We do not know what to do, but our eyes are upon you."
2 Chronicles 20:12

We receive many letters, email and telephone calls saying, "I do not know what to do regarding this circumstance or this problem." Many people, family and friends want to tell you what you should do. There is only ONE person that knows for certain what is going on in the heavenlies and that is your Lord God. He created you and has a plan for your entire life. Even if you are on a detour road, He knows the way to get back on the right road!

Go to the Lord and seek His face and His will for your life. Do you know that the Lord's way is always the best way for you and your family? Many years ago, I did not believe that. Today through many different ways, I now know that His way is the **very best way and only way** regarding every part of my life including my emotional, my physical, my financial and my spiritual life. I pray that you will find this out personally for yourself. Listen for his soft voice.

"My sheep listen to my voice; I know them and they follow me."
John 10:27

But I gave them this command: Obey me, and I will be your God and you will be my people. Walk in all the ways I command you, that it may go well with you.
Jeremiah 7:23

May you be encouraged today regarding **all the scriptures** below showing you **He wants to guide your every step.**

"...He will instruct him in the way chosen for him."

Psalm 25:12

"If you are pleased with me, teach me your ways so I may know you and continue to find favor with you."

Exodus 33:13

"If any of you lacks wisdom, he should ask God who gives generously to all without finding fault, and it will be given to him."

James 1:5

"Teach me to do your will, for you are my God; may your good Spirit lead me on level ground."

Psalm 143:10

"Choose my instruction instead of silver, knowledge rather than choice gold, for wisdom is more precious than rubies, and nothing you desire can compare with her."

Proverbs 8:10-11

"I desire to do you will, O my God; your law is within my heart."

Psalm 40:8

May you surrender your life to your Lord and Savior daily. May you remember when Jesus cried to His Heavenly Father in the Garden of Gethsemane, may that be your cry today.

"My Father, if it is possible, may this cup be taken from me. Yet not as I will, but as you will."

Matthew 26:39

Now go spend time with the Lord. Ask Him for His

direction in your life. Listen and then follow His instructions completely. Yes, you may be given the assignment to pray and fight the enemy for your spouse and loved one's souls. May you consider this a privilege and honor to serve the Lord. May you not be passive, but aggressive and tenacious in your warfare praying.

DO YOU HAVE HOPE?

May the God of hope fill you with all joy and peace as you trust in him, so that you may overflow with hope by the power of the Holy Spirit.

Romans 15:13

This is our prayer for each stander and prodigal today. May our God of hope fill each of you with joy and peace. Your God is a **God of HOPE**. I am afraid that many of you have lost your hope and are ready to give up, choosing to believe satan's lies and not God's truths.

Yet this I call to mind and therefore I have hope: Because of the Lord's great love we are not consumed, for his compassions never fail. They are new every morning; great is your faithfulness. I say to myself, "The Lord is my portion; therefore I will wait for him." The Lord is good to those whose hope is in him, to the one who seeks him; it is good to wait quietly for the salvation of the Lord.

Lamentations 3:21-26

Have you lost your hope in your God today? Have you lost your hope in life today? Have you lost your hope in your spouse, in your marriage, in your family, in your church or even your pastor? I know many of you are very close to that point. Many of you are depressed and oppressed. I pray as you read these scriptures, the Lord will speak to your inner man that your Lord God can lift you out of the deep hole of circumstances that you are in. Ask the Holy Spirit to touch your heart, your mind, your will and your emotions right now to receive God's truth! Our Lord God is a **GOD OF HOPE!**

"Find rest, O my soul, in God alone; my hope comes from him. He alone is my rock and my salvation; he is my fortress, I will not be shaken. My salvation and my honor depend on God; he

is my mighty rock, my refuge. Trust in him at all times, O people; pour out your hearts to him, for God is our refuge."
Psalm 62:5-8

Why are you downcast, O my soul? Why so disturbed within me? Put your hope in God, for I will yet praise him, my Savior and my God.
Psalm 42:5

Praise the Lord for God's Word. There is power in God's Word. Read God's Word daily, meditate on God's Word, study God's Word and memorize God's Word.

What is "Hope?" In the Bible dictionary it is *"confident expectancy."* In the Bible, the word HOPE stands for both the act of hoping and the things hoped for. Webster's Dictionary reads: *"a feeling that what is wanted will happen; desire accompanied by expectation. The things that one has a hope for. A reason for hope. A person or thing on which one may base some hope. Trust, Reliance."*

Praise the Lord, give me HOPE! **My prayer is that each of you will have CONFIDENT EXPECTANCY--HOPE!** Genuine hope is not wishful thinking, but a firm assurance about things that are unseen and still in the future.

Now faith is being sure of what we hope for and certain of what we do not see.
Hebrews 11:1

What are you hoping for? Is your hope for your spouse to know the Lord? Is your hope to have your spouse return home and rebuild your marriage on the solid rock of Jesus Christ? Is your hope to have all your loved ones to be saved? Believe in your Lord God! He wants the best for you, your spouse and your loved ones. Do not give up on God! He sent His Son to die on the cross for all sinners including your loved ones. Do not look at your present circumstances. Put your hope in the

Word of God!

May those who fear you rejoice when they see me, for I have put my hope in your word.

Psalm 119:74

Do you not know? Have you not heard? The Lord is the everlasting God, the Creator of the ends of the earth. He will not grow tired or weary, and his understanding no one can fathom. He gives strength to the weary and increases the power of the weak. Even youths grow tired and weary, and young men stumble and fall; but those who hope in the Lord will renew their strength. They will soar on wings like eagles; they will run and not grow weary, they will walk and not be faint.

Isaiah 40:28-31

For in this hope we were saved. But hope that is seen is no hope at all. Who hopes for what he already has? But if we hope for what we do not yet have, we wait for it patiently.

Romans 8:24-25

May the God of hope fill you with all joy and peace as you trust in him, so that you may overflow with hope by the power of the Holy Spirit.

Romans 15:13

The Lord delights in those who fear him, who put their hope in his unfailing love.

Psalm 147:11

Ask Him to fill you with all joy and peace so that you may overflow with HOPE by the power of the Holy Spirit. Now, believe, and He will do it!!

SEARCH ME, O GOD!

Search me, O God, and know my heart, test me and know my anxious thoughts. See if there is any offensive way in me, and lead me in the way everlasting.

Psalm 139:23-24

You need to go to your Heavenly Father and say "Search Me, O God! I know I have sinned and still sin against You. Search my heart and forgive me." If you will be honest with yourself, the Lord may have already shown you areas where you know that you played a part in your marriage falling apart. Your spouse may be very critical, judgmental, or he/she may have a bad temper, have fits of rage or even be involved in using alcohol or drugs. Regardless of the circumstances that you live in, through the power of the Holy Spirit, you do not have to react "in the flesh" and behave improperly. You can react as Jesus would and live with the power of the Holy Spirit living within you. You can demonstrate the fruits of the Holy Spirit. Your spouse may be very hard on you at the present time. I know that you are trying to please them, keep peace in your home and become the loving spouse. Ask the Lord to give you strength and Your Lord will deliver you out of your troubles.

Often Bob would ask me not to do something and unconsciously I would do it. If he was upset or would discipline the children unfairly, I put up the silent wall around me for the rest of the evening, regardless, of what he said after the children went to bed. That is not the way that Jesus would have reacted or behaved. The Lord started to reveal to me the areas in my life that needed to be changed first. Ask the Lord to forgive you for your sins and bad habits and ask Him to do a spiritual inventory of your heart.

For I know my transgressions, and my sin is always before me.

Against you, you only, have I sinned and done what is evil in your sight....

Psalm 51:3-4

After you spend time with the Lord, ask Him to show you areas of sinfulness or sins that you may not even know need to be confessed, forgiven and forgotten. When I started my *Spiritual Journey* many years ago, I asked the Lord to reveal to me if there were any deep, hidden sins in my life, or unforgiveness. To my surprise, the Lord brought current events as well as past events to my memory. He reminded me of an incident in my childhood and He asked me to forgive some children that had hurt and wounded me as a child.

Were you abused or wounded as a child? Statistics are very high showing that many children have been and are being sexually molested. If you were, you need to be healed by your Heavenly Father. Abuse as a child can cause damage to the body, to the mind, and to the emotions. It may cause you not to be able to love and trust your spouse. That is why I would like you to ask the Lord to search your heart and allow Him to be the Great Counselor and the Great Physician in your life. He can help you and show you how you can forgive ones that have hurt you so badly. You can learn to give your past to the Lord and lay everything in God's hands and allow Him to be the one who will deal, discipline and be the one to take vengeance on that person. All you need to do is forgive that person, let go and let God do the rest. Ask the Lord to give you the spirit of forgiveness in your heart. Ask the Lord to come and heal your wounded broken heart. Forgiveness is an act and a process. Your heart can be transformed by your Lord God starting today.

Know for certain that unforgiveness is hurting you more than it is affecting the person that has hurt you. Unforgiveness can lead to bitterness, hatred, hostility, anger and fear. Unforgiveness can destroy a person. It is also blocking and stopping your spiritual maturity.

You may not have enough time today to spend with the Lord and to have Him reveal hidden areas in your life. Tell Him you are willing to cleanse all the areas in your life. Ask Him to start preparing your heart to receive all that He wants to reveal to you.

If we claim to be without sin, we deceive ourselves and the truth is not in us. If we confess our sins, he is faithful and just and will forgive us our sins and purify us from all unrighteousness.

I John 1:8-9

Get a pad of paper or a journal to start writing different things the Lord will start revealing to you.

Create in me a pure heart, O God, and renew a steadfast spirit within me.

Psalm 51: 10

I, even I, am he who blots out your transgressions, for my own sake, and remembers your sins no more.

Isaiah 43:25

This is a very important step in your *Spiritual Journey*. If you are going to deepen your relationship with your Lord, you must not have areas that will block your personal relationship with your Heavenly Father.

How many wrongs and sins have I committed? Show me my offense and my sin.

Job 13:23

Have mercy on me, O God, according to your unfailing love; according to your great compassion blot out my transgressions. Wash away all my iniquity and cleanse me from my sin.

Psalm 51:1-2

Dear friend, take off your mask and be honest with yourself and with God. He knows everything about you. He knows all that you have done throughout your life. Your Lord God knows what you are thinking about your spouse and what you do and say all the time. Stop pretending, and cleanse yourself from your sins. May I suggest some areas that may need to be considered. You may have had premarital sex, an abortion, or cohabited with someone. You may have been involved with witchcraft, yoga, tarot cards, or worshiping other gods, not knowing the consequences of any of these sins. Ask the Lord to cleanse you from all your impurities and idols.

Some of you need to pray against generational curses from your parents, grandparents, and great grandparents. You may be reaping seeds that were sown years ago. Break the generational curses by the Blood and the Cross of your Lord Jesus Christ. He can break all soul ties that you had or your spouse is having by the Blood and the Cross of your Lord Jesus Christ. Your Lord can deliver you and your spouse from any and all sins. Nothing is too hard for Him. Then choose everyday to live a Christ-centered life.

Allow the Holy Spirit to do spiritual heart surgery. Do not blame others, as we often tend to do. Let's be honest and pray, *"Search me, O God, and remove everything not of you."*

"I will sprinkle clean water on you, and you will be clean; I will cleanse you from all your impurities and from all your idols. I will give you a new heart and put a new spirit in you; I will remove from you your heart of stone and give you a heart of flesh.

Ezekiel 36:25-26

CHANGE ME, LORD!

When you ask God to cleanse you from your impurities, you are saying to Him, "Forgive me, and change me, Lord." Part of being changed by God means that you must repent. To *repent* means **to change - to turn around 180 degrees. To repent of our sins means to forsake them - to willingly surrender our entire life to the One who created us.** Every person who wants eternal life must repent, turning away from their sins and changing their behavior. *"For all have sinned and fall short of the glory of God."* **Romans 3:23** You do not have to be a bad person, the Lord teaches us in the Bible that repentance is not an option, it is a command from God. Each of us have a free will, we all have the ability to choose between right and wrong. God is going to judge us accordingly. **Have you chosen to turn from your sins?**

Jesus answered...But unless you repent, you too shall perish.
Luke 13:2-3

Repent, then, and turn to God, so that you sins may be wiped out.....
Acts 3:19

If we confess our sins, he is faithful and just and will forgive us our sins and purify us from all unrighteousness.
I John 1:9

You cannot change by yourself. Your flesh is weak. You may be tempted to go back to your old ways and habits, without God's help. *BUT WITH GOD, WITH THE POWER OF THE HOLY SPIRIT,* He will change you from the inside out. There have been thousands of stories, for centuries, of sinners crying out, and being delivered from alcohol, drugs, pornography, adultery, overeating, smoking and cursing, etc. Do you want to be set free from the bondages of sin? Be honest before God and yourself. You must say, "Cleanse me, forgive me, and change me."

Many people you know and love say, "I believe You, Lord, *but* I do not want to give up my fun and sin right now. Later on I will get right with You." That is where so many of the prodigal spouses and our rebellious teenagers who are living in sin are right now. Most of them know they need to change, but at this present moment they do not want to turn away from the temporary high they are receiving from living in sin.

Our two sons work with the Medical Examiner's office. Bob was a Funeral Director and did this work before them. Each day they transport many people who have died suddenly or unexpectedly. Their families can testify that none of them expected to die when they awoke on the day of their death, but they did. If it were possible for any of these people to utter one last prayer to God, just as they saw Him, I know that it would be to repent.

For the wages of sin is death, but the gift of God is eternal life in Christ Jesus our Lord.

Romans 6:23

Do not compromise! Are you living in sin? Then repent now! Stop sinning! Our Lord God is a Holy, awesome God, a jealous God and a just God. Our prodigals play with fire everyday and gamble that they will not get burned. But they are being burned each day, although they will not admit it! Our prodigals do not want to admit that they are burning their spouses, their children and so many loved ones of the extended family.

Read the parable in **Luke 16:27-29** about the rich man who had everything in this world. Listen to his cry for his family:

...'Then I beg you, father, send Lazarus to my father's house, for I have five brothers. Let him warn them, so that they will not also come to this place of torment.' "Abraham replied, 'They have Moses and the Prophets; let them listen to them.'

Luke 16:27-29

... "I am the way and the truth and the life. No one comes to the Father except through me...."

John 14:6

There are grave and deep consequences to sin, especially continuous, habitual sin! People, I am writing this in love and pleading with each of you to pray for your loved ones and for **ALL prodigals**. Our prodigals are fantastic, wonderful people. Unfortunately, they fell into temptation and sin, and they do not see or believe that there is a way out. There is! **Jesus is the way, the truth and the light!** He will guide them out!

"...but I gave them this command: Obey me, and I will be your God and you will be my people. Walk in all the ways I command you, that it may go well with you. But they did not listen or pay attention; instead, they followed the stubborn inclinations of their evil hearts. They went backward and not forward."

Jeremiah 7:23-24

Stander, be honest with yourself. Have you during this time behaved in an ugly way or acted as a carnal Christian? You have allowed sin to come into your own lives *BECAUSE* of your spouse and all the circumstances. You blamed them, let's blame the right one--the enemy that has tempted you also--a different way. You fell and sinned in a different way, but SIN IS SIN. Let's repent, turn, change, and be filled with the Holy Spirit; who empowers you to live a Christlike life each and every day regardless of your circumstances.

The enemy is after the church and God's people. That is

why the church has a higher divorce rate than the world. Let's stop handing over to the enemy (satan) our pastors, our music leaders, our youth leaders, our missionaries, our deacons, our Sunday School teachers, our leaders, and our church family. Let's proclaim there is another way! Let's fight for all these good people who have fallen and have been taken captive by the enemy. These are God's children who need to come back to Him-NOW!

Let's go on this *Spiritual Journey*, asking the Holy Spirit to change you. Then choose to be a lighthouse for your Lord Jesus Christ. If you are going to say you are a Christian, let's be different, as Jesus taught us to be. "Lord, change me. I surrender my life to You."

Be imitators of God, therefore, as dearly loved children and live a life of love, just as Christ loved us and gave himself up for us as a fragrant offering and sacrifice to God.
Ephesians 5:1-2

A PRAYER FOR YOU TO PRAY

Lord, forgive me of all of my sins. Change me, mold me, melt me into the new creature in Christ that You want me to be. Lord, I cannot restore, rebuild or reconcile our marriage, but You can. I give you my life to be used by You. I choose to become an intercessor for all prodigals and children who have fallen into sin. I pray that You will teach me more about Your unconditional love and forgiveness for all Your children everyday. Thank You for forgiving me and starting the process of changing me to become the woman/man of God You desire for me to be. *Amen.*

FILL ME UP!

... "Do not leave Jerusalem, but wait for the gift my Father promised, which you have heard me speak about. For John baptized with water, but in a few days you will be baptized with the Holy Spirit."

Acts 1:4-5

May your prayer today be, "Fill me up Lord. I want more of you!" Sit in His presence and spend time with Him. Ask Him to fill you up to overflowing with the Holy Spirit. Through my crisis of Bob leaving our family, I surrendered my life, my will, my emotions, and my feelings to my Lord. I gave Him my life to do with as He chose. Our church had an altar where I cried out to God, but you may use your bed or your chair for your altar. Many of you know when you have had another encounter with your Lord, being filled with the Holy Spirit as spoken about in Acts.

Peter replied, "Repent and be baptized, every one of you, in the name of Jesus Christ for the forgiveness of your sins. And you will receive the gift of the Holy Spirit. The promise is for you and your children and for all who are far off--for all whom the Lord our God will call."

Acts 2:38-39

As you begin this *Spiritual Journey*, ask and allow the Holy Spirit to give you the power, the grace and the mercy to be able to start to change the areas that need to be changed. Ask the Holy Spirit to continue to show you daily what he wants to change in you and to create in you a new heart. Ask Him daily to examine and control your heart, your tongue, your emotions and your feelings. To show you areas that you need to allow the Holy Spirit to cleanse you from, any and all impurities, unrighteousness and from all idols. Let your personal goal be to act and react "like Jesus would." You can not do this yourself by your carnal flesh, but by the fruits of the Holy Spirit, which will empower you to do so.

But the fruits of the spirit is love, joy, peace, patience, kindness, goodness, faithfulness, gentleness and self-control...Those who belong to Christ Jesus have crucified the sinful nature with its passions and desires...Since we live by the Spirit, let us keep in step with the Spirit.

Galatians 5:22-23,25

...Instead, be filled with the Spirit. Speak to one another with psalms, hymns and spiritual songs. Sing and make music in your heart to the Lord, always giving thanks to God the Father for everything, in the name of our Lord Jesus Christ. Submit to one another out of reverence for Christ.

Ephesians 5:18-21

The Holy Spirit is with you each and every moment of your day. May you ask Him for His direction and His help for every problem of your day. Meditate on these scriptures to come to know the power of your Lord God. May you come to know that He does want to speak to you, directing your every step.

I will praise the Lord, who counsels me; even at night my heart instructs me. I have set the Lord always before me. Because he is at my right hand, I will not be shaken....You have made known to me the path of life; you will fill me with joy in your presence, with eternal pleasures at your right hand.

Psalm 16:7-8,11

Many of you are going through deep waters. I want to challenge you to cry out to your Lord God. Ask Him for a new touch, ask Him to fill you up with faith, hope and love beyond your understanding. Ask Him to reveal to you His will for your life today. Bob and I pray:

May the God of hope fill you with all joy and peace as you

-42-

trust in him, so that you may overflow with hope by the power of the Holy Spirit.

Romans 15:13

Our second prayer is that your spouse and ALL prodigals will be touched as Ananias touched Saul after the Damascus Road encounter with God. Read **Acts 9.** Pray that your spouse will have a Damascus Road experience and be changed completely. Saul's experience changed his life!

Then Ananias went to the house and entered it. Placing his hands on Saul, he said, "Brother Saul, the Lord--Jesus, who appeared to you on the road as you were coming here--has sent me so that you may see again and be filled with the Holy Spirit." Immediately, something like scales fell from Saul's eyes, and he could see again. He got up and was baptized,....

Acts 9:17-18

Be filled with the Holy Spirit-you and your family! Nothing is impossible or too hard for your God!

WHO IS YOUR GIANT?

Do you have a **GIANT** in your life? Do you have circumstances that seem overwhelming? Many standers who are going through separation and divorce feel there are many giants that are trying to kill, steal and destroy them or their family. What giant is bothering or tormenting you? Which giant is coming after you and your family? Is it the giant of separation, giant of divorce, giant of non-covenant marriage, giant of a pregnancy, giant of illness, giant of finances, giant of jealousy, giant of unforgiveness, giant of unbelief, giant of suicide, or giant of court hearings?

What does our Lord say about our giants as you continue your *Spiritual Journey*? Read **I Samuel 17.**

David's victory over Goliath came as a result of his faith in God that had already been tested and proven in his life. David knew His Lord. **David did not doubt or have unbelief that his God would always win**.

"The Lord who delivered me from the paw of the lion and the paw of the bear will deliver me from the hand of this Philistine."

I Samuel 17:37

Are you like David or like the Israelites? What caused David to not be afraid of the giant, Goliath? David had a heart for God. He always sought the Lord. David had a deep concern for the honor and reputation of the Lord God of Israel. Goliath was not just defying the armies of Israel, but the Lord Almighty. David had complete confidence in the Lord's power because of his previous encounters with big problems and situations as a shepherd. He personally knew God could deliver him from the enemy. **David trusted in God, not in himself.** The Spirit of the Lord came upon him in power.

David said to the Philistine, "You come against me with sword and spear and javelin, but I come against you in the name of the Lord Almighty, the God of the armies of Israel, whom you have defied...All those gathered here will know that it is not by sword or spear that the Lord saves; for the battle is the Lord's, and he will give all of you into our hands."

I Samuel 17:45,47

Become a David, put your complete trust and faith into your awesome mighty Lord. Do not be like the Israelites, full of fear. Believe in the power of the Holy Spirit. Believe what the Lord says to you will happen in His timing. Let the Lord get rid of your giants!

...'Not by might nor by power, but by my Spirit,' says the Lord Almighty.

Zechariah 4:6

REMEMBER SAUL!

Many of you ask, "How can I believe that God can change my spouse when my spouse says, 'I will never, never come back. I have never really loved you. I have put this off for years. You need to get on with your life as I am with mine. I do not care what God or the Bible says, you can not change my mind.'"

Bob and I cannot possibly write all the words that a prodigal will say to destroy all hope or faith in order that you will stop trying to change their mind or heart to return home. Bob and I understand why so often we receive mail and emails questioning, due to your personal circumstances, "Should I just get on with my life and give up?"

I want to encourage you that as we talk to standers, you share that the Lord actually showed you our Web page or someone else referred you to us. The Lord is trying to direct your path to accept an assignment for your family. I believe He is asking each of you to become an intercessor for your spouse and then for all the prodigals around the world who are in the far country living a life of sin. God can and does touch men and women to start a *Spiritual Journey* with Him today. God created you and sent His Son, Jesus, to die on the cross for all sinners.

Don't give up! God is moving every day in different ways. Just keep growing and maturing in the Lord. Please be burdened and continue to pray for everyone in your family to be saved.

"...What must I do to be saved?"..."Believe in the Lord Jesus, and you will be saved--you and your household."
Acts 16:30-31

Read the story of Paul in **Acts 25 and 26** for your

devotion today. Paul was allowed to speak in front of King Agrippa to testify why he should be set free. Paul was able to share his testimony of what happened to him on the Damascus Road. He told King Agrippa of his encounter with Jesus. Saul was chosen by Jesus and God to become an ambassador for the Gentiles.

Jesus said to Saul, "Now get up and stand on your feet. I have appeared to you to appoint you as a servant and as a witness of what you have seen of me and what I will show you. I will rescue you from your own people and from the Gentiles."

Acts 26:16

I am certain that any and all prodigals who have returned home (and there are many), are very thankful that their spouse did not give up on them! Don't give up on your spouse! God is able! Let's pray a scripture for your spouses that I discovered again today. It is so powerful and is found in **Acts 26:18.**

A PRAYER FOR YOU

Lord, we pray this for every prodigal who is away from You. We pray this for every spouse and every rebellious teenager who is in the pigpen of life and away from their family: "Lord, open their eyes and turn them from darkness to light and from the power of satan to God, so that they may receive forgiveness of sins and a place among those who are sanctified by faith in me. Thank you Lord for Your Word. What an awesome scripture! What powerful words! Lord, go and bring your prodigals home quickly. Nothing is too hard for you. In Jesus Name. *Amen.*

HE CARES FOR YOU

"Cast all your anxiety on him because he cares for you."
I Peter 5:7

There are many of you who have very **BIG** and real problems and **BIG** mountains in your life. May I reassure you that your Lord God is able to handle them ALL. He will never fail you. He is able to handle everything! Today give Him **ALL** your burdens.

...*"Never will I leave you; never will I forsake you." So we say with confidence, "The Lord is my helper; I will not be afraid. What can man do to me?"*
Hebrews 13:5-6

"Do not be anxious about anything, but in everything in prayer and petition, with thanksgiving, present your requests to God. And the peace of God, which transcends all understanding, will guard your hearts and your minds in Christ Jesus."
Philippians 4:6-7

This solution may sound very simplistic, but I know that it works. Try and give each problem that is weighing you down to the Lord. Tell the Lord that you are laying your problem at the foot of the cross and leave it there for the Lord to fix it, solve it or to remove it. Allow Him to be the Repairer or Counselor to all your problems.

"Commit your way to the Lord; trust in him and he will do this."
Psalm 37:5

But I call to God, and the Lord saves me. Evening, morning and noon I cry out in distress, and he hears my voice...Cast your cares on the Lord and he will sustain you; he will never

let the righteous fall.
Psalm 55:16-17,22

If God created the heavens and the earth, He can handle any one and all of your problems. So often you worry and you become anxious. You try to solve the problems yourself. Your Lord God is waiting for you to ask Him to help you. You may have problems due to your disobedience or sins. If this is part of the problem, repent, say you are sorry, confess it to your Lord, talk to Him and He will forgive you. Many times some of your problems are due to your spouse's problems or sins.

All we can do is, "Tell it to Jesus." He will take care of you. He loves you more than anyone else. You need to increase your faith in the Lord God.

Go to **Matthew 6:25-34** and read one of my favorite scriptures.

"Therefore I tell you, do not worry about your life, what you will eat or drink; or about your body, what you will wear...Look at the birds of the air; they do not sow or reap or store away in barns, and yet your heavenly Father feeds them. Are you not much more valuable than they? Who of you by worrying can add a single hour to his life?...But seek first his kingdom and his righteousness, and all these things will be given to you as well."
Matthew 6:25-27,33

This scripture was given to me by my Lord on my journey sixteen years ago when I was responsible for all our bills and caring for our three children. I needed help and the Lord showed me His power, daily. I know that it may sound impossible, but my Lord God met ALL my needs. He became my Provider, my Counselor, my Friend, my Husband, and my Comforter. He never failed me. He cared about me and my family. He cares about you and your family. Go to Him today!

A BOBSERVATION

I am so blessed to be able to get up early and to read for the first time what my wife has written the evening before for *Charlyne Cares*. I pray that you will stand strong until your spouse knows the joy that I know in not simply living under the same roof, but living in the joy of a restored and healed marriage.

Today we will hear about standers' impossible circumstances. Tomorrow (or some day soon) we will hear how the Lord came through for each one. I enjoy writing fiction, but some of the ways the Lord moves the mountains for our people, I could never have imagined. Remember, God works best when nothing else can.

THE PROMISES OF GOD

As you are on your *Spiritual Journey*, I pray that you will start to hunger, thirst, meditate, and memorize scriptures that give you wisdom, hope and encouragement. They will increase your faith in the power and in the promises of God.

When you receive a promise from God, hang on to it, believe it. Write the scripture or promise down in your journal. Also, write it in your Bible, put the date next to the scripture and/or put the person's name next to it. You can walk through the deep waters of marriage problems because your Lord Jesus is carrying you in His arms.

... *"Fear not, for I have redeemed you; I have summoned you by name; you are mine. When you pass through the waters, I will be with you; and when you pass through the rivers, they will not sweep over you. When you walk through the fire, you will not be burned; the flames will not set you ablaze."*
Isaiah 43:1-2

Seek the Lord with all your heart every day. I read a book which helped me grow in the Lord many years ago.. It taught me that God does speak. *Rhema* is Greek for a specific word from God. You may be reading along in the Bible and suddenly a verse really speaks to your heart or you feel like the verse is leaping off the page. In either case a passage becomes so meaningful that you sense God is speaking to you. A *rhema* word is a promise that God has definite plans for a circumstance or problem in your life. Throughout my stand, my Lord, gave me *rhema* verses of scriptures that seemed to leap off the page while reading the Bible. When this happened, I dated the scripture and wrote a note regarding whom it was about, or wrote a note in my journal. If you were to look at my Bible, you would see dates throughout it. I can say some have come to pass, while others I am still waiting for with expectation.

God wants you to know Him. He wants you to know His promises and His power. Do you really believe? Ask Him to remove all your doubts, fears and unbelief. You have a choice! Are you willing to pay the price to believe for restoration of your marriage and for your spouse to become a man or woman of God? You are in a spiritual battle. Are you willing to fight and sacrifice for your spouse and other loved ones? I hope you are, because thousands of marriages could be restored if we will only persevere.

...faith comes from hearing the message, and the message is heard through the Word of Christ.
Romans 10:17

The Lord is not slow in keeping his promise, as some understand slowness. He is patient with you, not wanting anyone to perish, but everyone to come to repentance.
2 Peter 3:9

The promise is for you and your children and for all who are far off--for all whom the Lord our God will call.
Acts 2:39

Commit to the Lord whatever you do, and your plans will succeed.
Proverbs 16:3

There is no wisdom, no insight, no plan that can succeed against the Lord.
Proverbs 21:30

Many are the plans in a man's heart, but it is the Lord's purpose that prevails.
Proverbs 19:21

In his heart a man plans his course, but the Lord determines his steps.
Proverbs 16:9

But the plans of the Lord stand firm forever, the purposes of his heart through all generations.

Psalm 33:11

...If God is for us, who can be against us?

Romans 8:31

...he who began a good work in you will carry it on to completion until the day of Christ Jesus.

Philippians 1:6

When a man's ways are pleasing to the Lord, he makes even his enemies live at peace with him.

Proverbs 16:7

Woe to those who go to great depths to hide their plans from the Lord, who do their work in darkness and think, "Who sees us? Who will know?"

Isaiah 29:15

There is a way that seems right to a man, but in the end it leads to death.

Proverbs 14:12

May He give you the desire of your heart and make all your plans succeed.

Psalm 20:4

Aren't these scriptures powerful? Awesome! We can **STAND and BELIEVE** on the promises of God! Believe in the Word of God and in the Promises of God! If you are discouraged, may these scriptures give you hope, faith, and encouragement until you have the desire to make the commitment to become tenacious, enduring the price that it will cost you for a season. Then you will reap a restored marriage!

WHEN GOD MAKES A PROMISE!

...till what he foretold came to pass, till the word of the Lord proved him true.

Psalm 105:19

Read **Psalm 105.** God makes promises constantly throughout the Bible. He wants to see if His people will believe Him. You have a choice and a challenge--will you believe? God promises He will never leave you or forsake you. Do you believe Him when you are going through a raging storm or you are in the darkest time or hour of your life?

... "Never will I leave you; never will I forsake you."

Hebrews 13:5

When God gives you a promise by a dream, a vision, a prophetic word, a scripture from the Word of God, or a promise from God, you will need faith. When we receive a personal promise, it will be backed up by the Bible. You must have faith. You must believe and trust in God.

And without faith it is impossible to please God, because anyone who comes him must believe that he exists and that he rewards those who earnestly seek him.

Hebrews 11:6

So do not throw away your confidence; it will be richly rewarded. You need to persevere so that when you have done the will of God, you will receive what he has promised.

Hebrews 10:35-36

"But my righteous one will live by faith...."

Hebrews 10:38

If you are crying inside and are thinking, "I do not have

enough faith," don't worry, you only need a tiny amount.

He replied, "Because you have so little faith. I tell you the truth, if you have faith as small as a mustard seed, you can say to this mountain, 'Move from here to there' and it will move. Nothing will be impossible for you."

Matthew 17:20-21

Do not live by what you see. Do you believe in God? When God speaks, believe what He says, He will do it!

"...But if you can do anything, take pity on us and help us." "'If you can'?" said Jesus. "Everything is possible for him who believes." Immediately the boy's father exclaimed, "I do believe; help me overcome my unbelief!"

Mark 9:22-24

"If you believe, you will receive whatever you ask for in prayer."

Matthew 21:22

Every Christian will be tested and tried. In the end, you have to choose who you will believe. If you choose to be disobedient, you will have to take the test over again or go around the mountain again. Do you believe in the Lord or the enemy? Today, write the date down and journal your commitment to **BELIEVE AND TRUST IN YOUR MIGHTY AWESOME GOD!**

STOP DOUBTING AND BELIEVE!

As each of you have had your own trials and tribulations, may you continue to remember the very special day "Resurrection Sunday." This day in a Christian's life makes you be able to face the good and the bad days. It reminds each of us who has victory over death and the enemy. God defeated satan.

Many of you are facing large circumstances due to marriage problems, health problems, financial problems, employment problems, housing problems, legal problems, and children problems. What do you do? You cry out to your Lord God. He will hear your heart's cry. He knows your pain. Let Him reassure you that **He is still in control regardless how your circumstances look.**

Jesus appeared many times after His Resurrection to show many people that "He Was Alive." Disciples and people doubted the power of God then, as they do now. Dear people, you must believe in the power of your Lord God! You need to remember who He is. He is your Savior, Lord, Counselor, Comforter, and Physician.

There are many doubting Thomas's. Pray confessing your faults, and ask the Lord to forgive you for your doubt and unbelief. When you have doubt, you have unbelief and then fear will set in. Do not allow the enemy to attack you! Believe in God, your Lord Jesus Christ and the Holy Spirit!

Read **John 20:19-31.** What a powerful passage!

This story reminds me of our standers or family members who says, "I will not believe it." Then our Lord is so loving and patient, wanting to show us His power and His way.

...Though the doors were locked, Jesus came and stood among them and said, "Peace be with you!" Then he said to Thomas, "Put your finger here; see my hands. Reach out your hand and put it into my side. Stop doubting and believe."

John 20:26-27

Your Lord God is trying to say to each of you today-**STOP DOUBTING AND BELIEVE!** Believe in His power. Believe in His ways! Trust Him! He loves you and your family more than you do. He wants **ALL** prodigals to come back to Him and to their families!

Let's stop doubting. Remove any unbelief or fear. Believe in God's power!

Thomas said to him, "My Lord and my God!" Then Jesus told him, "Because you have seen me, you have believed; blessed are those who have not seen and yet have believed."

John 20:28-29

Be on your guard; stand firm in the faith; be men of courage; be strong.

I Corinthians 16:13

PSALM ONE

Blessed is the man who does not walk in the counsel of the wicked or stand in the way of sinners or sit in the seat of mockers. But his delight is in the law of the Lord, and on his law he meditates day and night. He is like a tree planted by streams of water, which yields its fruit in season and whose leaf does not wither. Whatever he does prospers.

Psalm 1:1-3

While on this *Spiritual Journey*, may each of you pray in agreement that your spouses will meditate on the Word day and night. *Whoa!* "That is a big order! My spouse acts like there is no God." That is the very reason why you are standing.

Read, meditate and study **Psalm 1.** This Psalm contrasts two kinds of people: the godly, and the ungodly. Your spouse may be unrepentant at this moment. That is why you and I are burdened. You stand in the gap pleading mercy and grace on the sinners that you love so much. May each of you be careful to not judge, lest you fall into a trap of the enemy. Do not be self-righteous, pray with humility.

"Do not judge, or you too will be judged. For in the same way you judge others, you will be judged, and with the measure you use, it will be measured to you."

Matthew 7:1-2

There are some consequences to sin even if sins are confessed or not confessed. The longer a prodigal stays in sin there will be larger consequences regardless of their repentance. That is why you need to pray for them daily. Study about David. **A person MUST change their heart and their lifestyle. REPENT means to turn from sin and change one's behavior.** Pray that your spouse and all prodigals will repent and be obedient to the Lord voice.

Not so the wicked! They are like chaff that the wind blows away. Therefore the wicked will not stand in the judgment, nor sinners in the assembly of the righteous.
Psalm 1:4-5

May the Lord have mercy on all our loved ones. Please continue to pray and fast for all prodigals who have refused to acknowledge their Lord and the sins in their life.

For the Lord watches over the way of the righteous, but the way of the wicked will perish.
Psalm 1:6

You will be blessed if you choose to follow our Lord Jesus Christ. Listen to His will and His way in your life.

A BOBSERVATION

Who wants to be a millionaire? Here is your final question.

"Why are you standing for the restoration of your marriage?"

- 1. To have my spouse back home with me.

- 2. I hurt so badly I can't stand being alone.

- 3. To prove that my prayers were answered.

- 4. So my prodigal mate will come back to Christ.

Get it right and your spouse can receive eternal life. Get it wrong and you walk away empty handed. What's your final answer?

JOSEPH--A MAN OF GOD!

As you continue on this *Spiritual Journey*, let's read about one man of God who truly followed his Lord God's ways. He paid a price for a season, but the Lord blessed him mightily in the end.

Have you read about Joseph in Genesis recently? I love to teach about Joseph. What a man of God! God had a plan for Joseph's life. In spite of many circumstances throughout his life, God used Joseph to save many people, including his father and the brothers who had tried to kill him years before. That is forgiveness!

The Lord will use you and your family as examples in the future. Are you willing to be like Joseph and to go through many circumstances in your life? Joseph was rejected and deserted by his brothers. He was sold into slavery. He ran from sexual temptation, but was put into jail even though he was innocent. Regardless of Joseph's circumstances, it says:

The Lord was with Joseph and he prospered, and he lived in the house of his Egyptian master. When his master saw that the Lord was with him and that the Lord gave him success in everything he did, Joseph found favor in his eyes and became his attendant....the Lord blessed the household of the Egyptian because of Joseph.

Genesis 39:2-5

What a verse of scripture! I worked for Cardiology Associates, my previous employer for twenty five years. I prayed for salvations and blessings for that business for many years. You should consider the impact you can have by praying for other people's salvation, as well as blessings on their activities.

When Joseph was asked to interpret a dream, Joseph's reply was:

"I cannot do it, "..." but God will give Pharaoh the answer he desires. "

Genesis 41:16

May you always ask for God's wisdom, knowledge and understanding for every circumstance in your life. Your ways are not His ways.

...it is the spirit in a man, the breath of the Almighty, that gives him understanding.

Job 32:8

Joseph and his brothers were reunited years later. God allowed Joseph to save his brothers and father from famine. May you have wisdom like Joseph as he realized that God allowed each circumstance to bring glory and honor to his God.

But Joseph said to them, "Don't be afraid. Am I in the place of God? You intended to harm me, but God intended it for good to accomplish what is now being done, the saving of may lives. So then, don't be afraid. I will provide for you and your children..... "

Genesis 50:19-21

What an example Joseph is for all of us! His brothers tried to destroy him, but years later Joseph forgave them and was used by God to help them. Lord, teach me Your ways!

ACTIONS SPEAK LOUDER THAN WORDS

As you continue your *Spiritual Journey* toward a healed family, may you ask the Lord to help you put into practice all that you are learning with Jesus Christ as your Teacher. Your co-workers, family, friends, and yes, even your spouse will start to see a difference in your words, as well your actions and reactions, even before they hear about a change in your heart. You must be different!

... 'Come and hear the message that has come from the Lord.' My people come to you, as they usually do, and sit before you to listen to your words, but they do not put them into practice. With their mouths they express devotion, but their hearts are greedy for unjust gain.

Ezekiel 33:30-31

Today, ask the Lord if you are putting into practice what you have been learning as a Christian. As you read and study the Bible, do you take the instructions, precepts and principles that your Lord teaches you and apply them to your personal life? Every day as you have your devotion time, ask the Lord to help you practice what you read and speak.

Dear children, let us not love with words or tongue but with actions and in truth.

I John 3:18

Do not merely listen to the word, and so deceive yourselves. Do what it says.

James 1:22

For it is not those who hear the law who are righteous in God's sight, but it is those who obey the law who will be declared righteous.

Romans 2:13

Who is wise and understanding among you? Let him show it by his good life, by deeds done in the humility that comes from wisdom.

James 3:13

They claim to know God, but by their actions they deny him.

Titus 1:16

Now that you know these things, you will be blessed if you do them.

John 13:17

May these scriptures encourage you to search your heart and be certain that you do not just read the Word, but put into practice and into action what your Lord is teaching you daily. Be careful that you do not become deceived. If you talk faith, you need to walk in faith. If you talk forgiveness, you need to walk in forgiveness. If you talk unconditional love, you need to walk in unconditional love.

"I will show you what he is like who comes to me and hears my words and puts them into practice. He is like a man building a house, who dug down deep and laid the foundation on rock. When a flood came, the torrent struck that house but could not shake it, because it was well built. But the one who hears my words and does not put them into practice is like a man who built a house on the ground without a foundation. The moment the torrent struck that house, it collapsed and its destruction was complete."

Luke 6:47-49

May each of you take heed to all these scriptures and be obedient to the Word of God. You need to apply and put into practice what you learn, what you believe and share about your Lord daily. **Action speaks louder than words!**

"ME? TEMPTED? NEVER!"

Do you not know that your body is a temple of the Holy Spirit, who is in you, whom you have received from God? You are not your own; you were bought at a price. Therefore honor God with your body.

I Corinthians 6:19-20

I pray that churches would start preaching against sexual immorality. Advertising and television demonstrate that the world is sliding into Hell through the bedroom, and we Christians are laughing at and ignoring what we are observing.

During your *Spiritual Journey*, you need to be especially aware of the schemes of satan to bring down your stand for your restored marriage through sexual immorality. You need to use caution and know what you would do if there was a temptation at work or at church.

Bob and I do not want to sound like experts, but we have heard over and over again, "It's all right because he/she is only a friend." Others will tell us, "I can handle it." We also hear, "It's not really a date because we are both standers."

We would be doing less than what God has called us to do if we failed to caution you about the perils of sexual temptation that await many standers, if you are not careful.

Most of you never thought there would have been unfaithfulness in your marriage. I know. I felt the same way when Bob and I were married.

Every married person needs to know the consequences of playing with dynamite. You will get burned. The first or second casual thought may seem harmless. The more the enemy has you thinking lustful thoughts, the more you and your loved ones will be harmed. Our spouses have been tempted, but beware you can also be tempted!

...The body is not meant for sexual immorality, but for the Lord, and the Lord for the body,...Do you not know that your bodies are members of Christ himself? Shall I then take the members of Christ and unite them with a prostitute? Never!
I Corinthians 6:13,15

May you always remember your marriage vows. Stand in the gap, waiting for the Lord to speak to your spouse, that they may come to their senses escaping from the enemy's camp.

But since there is so much immorality, each man should have his own wife, and each woman her own husband.
I Corinthians 7:2

May you and I always keep away from evil temptations. Recognize that the enemy will also try to tempt you during your stand. The enemy may tell you "to get on with your life," or the lie, "there is someone else better for you."

As you take this *Spiritual Journey* toward a restored home by standing with God for your marriage, you need to surrender your life to the Lord. That is the only way to resist sexual temptation when you are most vulnerable due to rejection by your spouse.

Therefore, prepare your minds for action; be self-controlled; set your hope fully on the grace to be given you when Jesus Christ is revealed. As obedient children, do not conform to the evil desires you had when you lived in ignorance. But just as he who called you is holy, so be holy in all you do; for it is written: "Be holy, because I am holy."
I Peter 1:13-16

A BOBSERVATION

We all know people who have given up their stand after they met someone they claim God has brought into their lives. There is one sure test of the new relationship being of God; "Does it involve sex?" If so, it is not of God.

But among you there must not be even a hint of sexual immorality; or of any kind of impurity, or of greed, because they are improper for God's holy people...For of this you can be sure: No immoral, impure or greedy person--such a man is an idolater--has any inheritance in the kingdom of Christ and God.

Ephesians 5:3,5

We each need to have a special burden for former standers who have fallen into this temptation. God does give His children second or third chances, so repent and start standing again.

BECOME BURDENED ABOUT SIN

You are in a spiritual battle! It started in Genesis Chapter Three with the Fall. There is a war going on night and day for the souls of men and women. There is a battle going on for the mind of your children. You need to know that the enemy is not your spouse, but satan.

"The thief comes only to steal and kill and destroy."
John 10:10

I am not only burdened about the sinfulness of our nation, but I am burdened about the sinfulness of all prodigals. They act and talk like strangers, someone you do not even know. The values and beliefs that they shared with their spouse and family have been thrown away for a different lifestyle. May you remember that the enemy has deceived them. They have been brainwashed into thinking evil is good.

May you and I never become weary in fighting this battle for the husbands, wives, fathers, mothers and all the young people in our families. Each person is a victim in the destruction of another family.

"Let us not become weary in doing good, for at the proper time we will reap a harvest if we do not give up."
Galatians 6:9

I know many of you write to us and say it is hopeless. Due to the constant negative words and actions, you feel that there is no evidence that the other person will ever *"come to their senses and escape from the trap of the devil."* **2 Timothy 2:26** Many of your friends and relatives are constantly telling you to "get on with your life." Your spouse does not want you, so why wait for them? They are planning their future lives without you and the children.

May I encourage you to:

"Do not be deceived: God cannot be mocked. A man reaps what he sows. The one who sows to please his sinful nature, from that nature will reap destruction; the one who sows to please the Spirit, from the Spirit will reap eternal life."
Galatians 6:7-8

What you are doing is standing in the gap for sinners. You are pleading their case before God. You are praying and interceding to your Lord Jesus Christ so He can become the deliverer of your spouse and other prodigals. Read **Luke 18:1-8.**

"Do you not know that the wicked will not inherit the kingdom of God? Do not be deceived: Neither the sexually immoral nor idolaters nor adulterers nor male prostitutes nor homosexual offenders nor thieves nor the greedy nor drunkards nor slanderers nor swindlers will inherit the kingdom of God. And that is what some of you were. But you were washed, you were sanctified, you were justified in the name of the Lord Jesus Christ and by the Spirit of our God."
I Corinthians 6:9-11

Cry out to your Lord and be burdened for your spouse's salvation. Ask the Lord what He wants you to do and then do it!! Become burdened for your spouse who is deceived and blinded by the enemy. Stand firm and pray, believing your Lord Jesus Christ will call your spouse's name, leaving the ninety-nine sheep to going after the one lost sheep. Do not give up on your spouse. Be burdened for their salvation. You may be the only one that will NOT stop praying for their soul.

"I tell you that in the same way there will be more rejoicing in heaven over one sinner who repents than over ninety-nine righteous persons who do not need to repent."
Luke 15:7

THE POWER OF PRAYER

"Call to me and I will answer you and tell you great and unsearchable things you do not know."
Jeremiah 33:3

May each of us learn to believe in the POWER OF PRAYER! I am truly convinced, that when you get to heaven, will you find out how you would have received many more miracles, if you had spent more time praying and talking to your Heavenly Father.

"Now to him who is able to do immeasurably more than all we ask or imagine, according to his power that is at work with us."
Ephesians 3:20

...The prayer of a righteous man is powerful and effective. Elijah was a man just like us. He prayed earnestly that it would not rain, and it did not rain on the land for three and a half years. Again, he prayed, and the heavens gave rain, and the earth produced its crops.
James 5:16-18

May you pray and believe like Elijah did. Do you believe God is moving behind the scenes when you are praying? I do! Over and over again, we hear of miracles because someone prayed earnestly. I believe more in prayer than anything else to bring your prodigal home or for answers to any and all of your circumstances.

I wish I had time to write a book on *"Answers to Prayers."* They are unbelievable. Anyone who knows Rejoice Ministry knows how much I believe in prayer. Bob being alive and well is due to the power of prayer, bringing glory and honor to our Lord. There are hundreds of answers to prayers since the Lord touched me in 1986 to pray for Bob and our family.

An example of something that seemed amazing to me was finding my white bag I had lost in New York City in 2001. Many already know the story, but we lost the white bag outside a New York hotel and everyone said it was gone forever! "You will never get anything back from New York City!" I told my friends, "You do not know my God!" God answered my prayer by delivering my lost bag to our home two days later. Now you know why I believe the Lord can bring any prodigal home!

As I reread the Gospels, I see Jesus teaching, but I also see Him praying to His Heavenly Father *ALL* the time. May you follow His example and be more like Him everyday.

"One day Jesus was praying in a certain place. When he finished, one of his disciples said to him, "Lord, teach us to pray..."

Luke 11:1

May you never give up praying for your loved ones and others. The Lord every day shows and reminds me to pray for certain people. Only when you get to heaven will you see how the Lord uses each of us to pray for prodigals and marriages.

"Pray continually; give thanks in all circumstances, for this is God's will for you in Christ Jesus."

I Thessalonians 5:17-18

Never stop praying and believing for miracles for all the prodigals throughout the land!

IS YOUR SPOUSE YOUR ENEMY?

Who is your enemy? Your spouse? Many would say, "Yes, because they_____, and they _____ and they are still_____ against me." I thought the same way many years ago. I could not believe that my husband would be unfaithful. I could not believe that my husband who loved our children would risk giving up everything for his own selfish desires. During my own *Spiritual Journey*, I found out who the enemy really was in our family.

For our struggle is not against flesh and blood, but against the rulers, against the authorities, against the powers of this dark world and against the spiritual forces of evil in the heavenly realms.

Ephesians 6:12

On your *Spiritual Journey*, I want you to become knowledgeable about the enemy, the devil.

You need to **beware** of the enemy as his **purpose** is to destroy all of us. You need to **be on guard or alert** against the enemy's attacks.

The thief comes only to steal and kill and destroy; I have come that they may have life, and have it to the full.

John 10:10

Be self-controlled and alert. Your enemy the devil prowls around like a roaring lion looking for someone to devour. Resist him, standing firm in the faith, because you know that your brothers throughout the world are undergoing the same kind of sufferings.

I Peter 5:8-9

Our Lord God has given us weapons to fight the enemy.

Learn to pray, fight the enemy and use the spiritual weapons:

- *Word of God: Read Hebrews 4:12, Ephesians 6:17*
- *The Name of Jesus: Read Matthew 28:18-20*
- *Armor of God: Read Ephesians 6:10-17*
- *Love: I Peter 4:8, I Corinthians 13:8,*
- *Hedge of Thornbushes: Read Hosea 2:6-7*
- *The Blood of the Lamb: Read Revelation 12:10-12*
- *Fasting: Read Isaiah 58:6*
- *Wall of Fire: 2 Kings 6:16-17*
- *Praise: Read Psalm 8:1-2*

Though we live in the world, we do not wage war as the world does. The weapons we fight with are not the weapons of the world. On the contrary, they have divine powers to demolish strongholds. We demolish arguments and every pretension that sets itself up against the knowledge of God, and we take captive every thought to make it obedient to Christ.

2 Corinthians 10:3-5

As you continue your *Spiritual Journey*, I challenge you to start reading more about spiritual warfare. Do not be afraid or fearful. God is on the throne. Walk in victory. Know who you are in Christ! There is victory for your prodigal and loved ones! Jesus Christ defeated the enemy, satan, through his death on the cross and His Resurrection three days later.

You. dear children, are from God and have overcome them, because the one who is in you is greater than the one who is in the world.

I John 4:4

"....I have given you authority to trample on snakes and scorpions and to overcome all the power of the enemy; nothing will harm you...."

Luke 10:19

Remember, your spouse is not your enemy. The enemy is satan. You have the authority through Jesus Christ to win the war for your family.

A BOBSERVATION

If it seems like you are meeting the enemy head-on everyday, rejoice that you are not going the same direction.

ARE YOU DRESSED IN THE MORNING?

I have had the Lord speak to my heart so strongly lately about our lack of knowledge.

My people are destroyed for lack of knowledge.
Hosea 4:6 NKJV

Do you put on the Armor of God on you and your family daily? We took a survey on our Cyperpoll and the results were not as I had hoped. The Statistics were: 56% Yes; 44% No. I believe 44% of standers are not understanding the importance of praying the Armor of God on themselves daily and it is dangerous for you, your spouse and your family. I want you to start learning about the Armor of God. I want you to understand the impact of wearing the Armor of God. You may not understand completely the first time. That is all right. Do not worry. God will teach you and give you more wisdom if you only ask.

If any of you lacks wisdom, let him ask of God, who gives to all liberally and without reproach, and it will be given to him.
James 1:5 NKJV

You need to understand, as I teach so often, that your marriage problems are not from your spouse but from the enemy. The scripture to emphasize this is:

Therefore take up the whole armor of God, that you may be able to withstand in the evil day, and having done all, to stand.
Ephesians 6:13 NKJV

Let me say this even more clearly. I am going to use the Living Bible. I use many translations in doing my studies. Many brand new Christians, who have had no exposure to church life, may want to start reading the Living Bible first, then go on to NIV translation or the NKJV. Each of you will have your own preference.

Last of all I want to remind you that your strength must come from the Lord's mighty power within you. Put on all of God's armor so that you will be able to stand safe against all strategies and tricks of Satan. For we are not fighting against people made of flesh and blood, but against persons without bodies--the evil rulers of the unseen world, those mighty satanic beings and great evil princes of darkness who rule this world; and against huge numbers of wicked spirits in the spirit world. So use every piece of God's armor to resist the enemy whenever he attacks, and when it is all over, you will still be standing up.

Ephesians 6:10-13 TLB

This armor is for your protection. God has given you very clear commands in the scriptures as to how to prepare for and face your conflict with the devil. You must learn how to resist the devil.

You must not be deceived. Your best protection against deception is growing in wisdom, knowledge and understanding, learning Biblical truths. Unfortunately, we still hear of church people and many Men of God falling into sin. Pray for your pastors and all Men of God! They need your prayers. Most of them, due to their position cannot admit to what is going on in their own personal lives.

Be self-controlled and alert. Your enemy the devil prowls around like a roaring lion looking for someone to devour. Resist him, standing firm in the faith....

I Peter 5:8-9

Paul tells us that we are to STAND FIRM against our spiritual enemies. The armor is made up entirely of spiritual weapons: Truth, Righteousness, Gospel of Peace, Faith, Salvation, Word of God and Prayer. You are going to learn to wear and to use these powerful weapons, so that you can *resist* the carefully laid plans of the devil. When the fight is over, you will still be standing!

Read **Ephesians 6:10-18.**

1.) Gird your loins with Truth--A girder supports - holds up. Always know and seek the truth about Christ and your relationship with Him.

2.) Put on the Breastplate of Righteousness-it protects your emotions, as you ask for the cleansing of guilt and your sins through Jesus' blood, accept and receive your forgiveness of your sins.

3.) Shod your feet with the preparation of the Gospel of Peace--allow the Peace of God to flood your mind, will and emotions.

4.) Take up the Shield of Faith--Our defense is faith, which quenches **all the arrows** of satan's plans and schemes against us today, in Jesus' name.

5.) Put on the Helmet of Salvation--This protects your thought process and your thinking. Know that the devil uses your mind for his battlefield.

6.) Take up the sword of the Spirit, which is the Word of God. This is your defense against the enemy's attacks. Jesus always responded, *"It is written...."*

Every day when you get up and get dressed for work or to play, be sure to put the Armor of God on yourself, your spouse and your family. (You do not know if one of your loved ones did not do it or is not spiritually right with God.)

Praise be to the Lord my rock, who trains my hands for war, my fingers for battle. He is my loving God and my fortress, my stronghold and my deliverer, my shield, in whom I take refuge, who subdues peoples under me.

Psalm 144:1-2

But the Lord is faithful, and he will strengthen and protect you from the evil one.

2 Thessalonians 3:3

You are in the Lord's army, be proud and be dressed for duty everyday! God is greater than any enemy!

PRAY--KNOWING YOUR AUTHORITY

Do you know who you are in Christ? You are a child of the King. You are an ambassador for Christ! The devil knows he is defeated, but we Christians walk around like we are the defeated ones.

The Lord left us with the Holy Spirit and power from on high. Why are you allowing the devil to destroy your family and loved ones? Let's pray with authority! Tell the devil, "It is written," like Jesus said to the evil one.

"For though we live in the world, we do not wage war as the world does. The weapons we fight with are not the weapons of the world. On the contrary, they have divine power to demolish strongholds."

2 Corinthians 10:3-4

"All this is from God, who reconciled us to himself through Christ and gave us the ministry of reconciliation...And he has committed to us the message of reconciliation. We are therefore Christ's ambassadors, as though God were making his appeal through us. We implore you on Christ's behalf: Be reconciled to God."

2 Corinthians 5:18-20

Use your weapons, the full Armor of God, which include: the belt of truth, the breastplate of righteousness, the gospel of peace, the shield of faith, the helmet of salvation, the sword of the spirit which is the Word of God; the Blood of Jesus, the hedge of thorns, the wall of fire, the joy of the Lord and the Name of Jesus.

Daily pray in authority knowing who you are in Christ. Bind the enemy, loose on your loved ones the fruits of the Holy Spirit and God's will in their lives. Pray for their salvation. Pray that their spiritual eyes and ears will be opened and that they will be revealed the truth by the Lord Jesus Christ. Pray for their repentance that they will come home to their Lord and family. **Read Luke 15**, the story of the Prodigal Son.

"When he came to his senses, he said, 'How many of my father's hired men have food to spare, and here I am starving to death! I will set out and go back to my father and say to him: Father, I have sinned against heaven and against you.
Luke 15:17-18

Pray that you will have at least one prayer partner. Not someone to share circumstances with, but an individual to pray for salvation and for God to move on your loved one's life. God will move mountains if we will only pray continually with perseverance and be tenacity.

Pray for your church, your pastor, your country, and all other prodigals and standers. YOUR PRAYER LIFE CAN MAKE A DIFFERENCE! IS IT DOING SO TODAY?

"Therefore I tell you, whatever you ask for in prayer, believe that you have received it, and it will be yours. And when you stand praying, if you hold anything against anyone, forgive him, so that your Father in heaven may forgive you your sins."
Mark 11:24-26

It will be exciting when you start to see God moving due to so many people praying for prodigals and families!

PRAY IN AGREEMENT!

"I tell you the truth, whatever you bind on earth will be bound in heaven, and whatever you loose on earth will be loosed in heaven. Again, I tell you that if two of you on earth agree about anything you ask for, it will be done for you by my Father in heaven. For where two or three come together in my name, there am I with them. "

Matthew 18:18-20

I am certain that there are many hundreds or thousands of families around the world that have a spouse speaking of separation and divorce today. Will you pray in agreement with a group of people called "standers," interceding for marriages daily, that your awesome, mighty God will intervene and start touching and changing the prodigal's hearts **BEFORE THEY EVER LEAVE home?** Praise the Lord for answered prayers.

We received an email which read: "Hello. I am writing to you with a heavy heart. My friend is going to leave her husband. They have three wonderful children and have been married for about 16 years. She thinks it is God's will for her to leave her husband. I told her this was not His will but she will not listen to me. I have been praying for her. She knows how I feel about this and I do not want to loose touch with her so I have backed off from telling her what the Bible says. I just do not know what to do. Please pray for her and if there is some literature I can give her please tell me what the titles are so I can get them for her. Thank you so much for your time and prayers."

I replied, "Thank you for writing. Please tell your friend about our ministry and how I divorced my husband. Do you know our story? Ask her if she would talk to me. Does she know the Lord?"

Today pray for the many families struggling with severe marriage problems at home and pray for each family who has a prodigal in the far country. Let's pray:

*"Lord, we come together in agreement where in **Matthew 18:19** we read that if two of you on earth agree about anything we ask for, it will be done for us by our Father in heaven. For where two or three come together in My name, there am I with them. Lord, we pray that no weapon formed against this family will prevail. Satan, you were defeated at the cross when our Lord Jesus Christ was crucified. He arose showing you His mighty power. Get away from this family and all families around the world who are speaking separation and divorce. God hates divorce, instead he will be the Repairer of Broken Walls, a Repairer of the Breech and will rebuild homes on the solid rock of Jesus Christ.*

"Lord, we are praying that both of these people and all our prodigals around the world will have a personal relationship with You as their Savior and as their Lord. For it is by grace that each of us has been saved through faith, not of ourselves, but a gift from God. Lord, we are putting the full armor of God on this family and on all the families around the world who have strife of separation going on in their homes, putting a hedge of protection and the blood of Jesus over them, so that we can take a stand against the devil's schemes. We stand in agreement with our Lord God and know that all of the enemy's tricks and schemes against this family and other families are broken.

"For our struggles are not against flesh and blood, but against the rulers, against the authorities, against the powers of this dark world and against the spiritual forces of evil in the heavenly realms. Lord, we pray that all the spouses who are planning on leaving and the ones who are gone will flee the evil desires of youth, and instead pursue righteousness, faith, love and peace, along with those who call on the Lord out of a pure heart. We pray that they will

come to their senses and escape from the trap of the devil, who has taken them captive to do his will. We know that Your sheep hear Your voice, so speak loudly to Your children today and we pray that they will be obedient to Your voice, Your will, and Your way.

"Lord, we praise You that You are in control of this crisis, and I pray that You will show Your people the power of prayer. Give hope to husbands and wives, showing them and speaking to them that You can heal, restore and rebuild their marriage. Nothing is too hard for You, and greater is He that is in us than he who is in the world.

*"Lord, we praise You and thank You that we have confidence in approaching You; that if we ask in anything according to Your will, You hear us. And we know that when You hear us-whatever we ask-we know that we have what we asked of You. I pray **I Corinthians 13:4-8** on them, restoring their love as the day each of them got married. Lord, we give this couple and all the other couples around the world to You Lord, and trust You to protect them from the evil one. We pray this in the mighty name of our Lord Jesus Christ. Amen"*

May you always remember to pray for other marriages, as well as for your own. May many prodigals TODAY be set free from satan's chains, coming home to their Lord God and their families now! Praise the Lord!

THE WALL OF FIRE

"So the king of Israel checked on the place indicated by the man of God. Time and again Elisha warned the king, so that he was on his guard in such places."

2 Kings 6:10

Many times in your stand, circumstances may come against you. May this story of Elisha encourage you, knowing that in the spiritual realm there are a hosts of ministering angels active in the lives of God's people.

Read **2 Kings 6:8-23.**

A PRAYER FOR YOU

Lord, You are the teacher. Speak to Your children today regarding their circumstances and give them the Word of Encouragement that they need to hear from You. *Amen.*

None of us, my lord the king," said one of his officers "but Elisha, the prophet who is in Israel, tells the king of Israel the very words you speak in your bedroom." "Go, find out where he is," The king ordered, "So I can send men and capture him.

2 Kings 6:12-13

Today, regardless of who is coming against you, remember the awesome power of your God.

"When the servant of the man of God got up and went out early the next morning, an army with horses and chariots had surrounded the city. "Oh, my lord, what shall we do?" The servant asked."

2 Kings 6:15

Always go to the Lord and ask Him what you should do

regarding any circumstance or problem that is coming against you. Seek the Lord for His answer only.

"Don't be afraid," The prophet answered. "Those who are with us are more than those who are with them." And Elisha prayed, "O Lord, open his eyes so he may see." Then the Lord opened the servant's eyes, and he looked and saw the hills full of horses and chariots of fire all around Elisha."

2 Kings 6:16-17

Often I pray a wall of fire around my family to protect them from the evil one. I have also prayed that my Lord will open my family's spiritual eyes to see the power of God.

"'And I myself will be a wall of fire around it,' declares the Lord, 'and I will be its glory within.'"

Zechariah 2:5

As you read this Bible story, look at some principles you can learn today:

1) There are a host of ministering angels who are active in the lives of God's people.

"Then no harm will befall you, no disaster will come near your tent. For he will command his angels concerning you to guard you in all your ways."

Psalm 91:10-11

2) Remember who is on your side.

"....If God is for us, who can be against us?"

Romans 8:31

3) Pray that God would deliver you and your loved ones from spiritual blindness. Pray that the eyes of each of their hearts will be opened to see the Truth.

I pray also that the eyes of your heart may be enlightened in order that you may know the hope to which he has called you, the riches of his glorious inheritance in the saints, and his incomparably great power for us who believe.

Ephesians 1:18-19

"Then you will know the truth, and the truth will set you free."

John 8:32

There is power in the Holy Spirit. Pray that the Holy Spirit will move in on your spouse. Bind the enemy so that your spouse can see and hear from the Holy Spirit.

"Ah, Sovereign Lord, you have made the heavens and the earth by your great power and outstretched arm. Nothing is too hard for you."

Jeremiah 32:17

Pray that thousands of prodigals will hear and see the power of God, repenting, turning away from their sinful lifestyle and come back to their Lord and to their families!

LORD, CHANGE OUR HEARTS!

Most marriage problems could be solved by each spouse allowing their heart to be touched by our Lord Jesus Christ. Have you allowed the Lord to touch your heart completely? What about your spouse's heart? If your loved one's heart has not been touched by God, their heart is sinful.

"The good man brings good things out of the good stored up in his heart, and the evil man brings evil things out of the evil stored up in his heart. For out of the overflow of his heart his mouth speaks."

Luke 6:45

"The heart is deceitful above all things and beyond cure. Who can understand it? "I the Lord search the heart and examine the mind, to reward a man according to his conduct, according to what his deeds deserve."

Jeremiah 17:9-10

The heart of stone cannot be changed by itself. The only way to experience God's love, grace and mercy is to be born again through faith in Jesus Christ and to receive a new heart. A new heart hates evil and delights in doing God's will.

The heart is the center of our being. It determines our inner and outward behavior. Our heart is the center of our intellect, the center of our emotions and the center of our human will.

Have you allowed your Lord Jesus Christ to change your heart? Do you or your spouse have a heart of flesh or a heart of stone? Before you criticize your spouse's heart, may you be certain that you have dealt with your own heart first. Allow the Lord to touch and change your heart first.

Do you need a heart transplant today? Do you need God's

love infused into your body? Has your heart become cold or unresponsive? Then let the Holy Spirit give you a cardioversion from the Great Physician. May your prayer be today that you, your spouse and your loved ones will allow God to guard and cleanse your hearts. Do not procrastinate any longer.

Above all else, guard your heart, for it is the wellspring of life.

Proverbs 4:23

Create in me a pure heart, O God, and renew a steadfast spirit within me.

Psalm 51:10

"I will give them a undivided heart and put a new spirit in them;...."

Ezekiel 11:19

"...Repent! Turn away from all your offenses; then sin will not be your downfall. Rid yourselves of all the offenses you have committed, and get a new heart and a new spirit."

Ezekiel 18:30-31

"'I will sprinkle clean water on you, and you will be clean; I will cleanse you from all your impurities and from all your idols. I will give you a new heart and put a new spirit in you; I will remove from you your heart of stone and give you a heart of flesh.'"

Ezekiel 36:25-26

Pray and spend some time with the Lord today so that you may re-examine your heart and pray that your prodigal will repent and allow the Holy Spirit to touch and change their hearts.

You can pray many of the above scriptures with your spouse's name in them. There is power in praying scriptures with your family member's name in them. Then, in God's awesome way, He will start changing their heart and they will turn away from their sinful lifestyle. Remember, when your prodigal comes home, be sure to give God all the glory!

WAIT FOR YOUR SPOUSE!

Let us not become weary in doing good, for at the proper time we will reap a harvest if we do not give up.

Galatians 6:9

Bob and I hurt the most when we receive a letter from a stander who writes to tell us, or implies that, "I am not going to stand for my marriage any longer. Oh, I will still pray for my spouse, but I have to 'get on with my life.' It is not good to hurt for so long and everyone around me knows that my spouse says that they will never ever come home. I love your ministry, but I am not certain that God will bring my spouse home."

I get so mad at the devil when I hear comments like that! Why? Because the enemy just deceived the stander as well as the spouse! Why do Christians believe that their Lord God cannot save, set free or deliver their spouse from the bondages of sin or deliver them from the trap of the satan?

...in the hope that God will grant them repentance leading them to a knowledge of the truth, and that they will come to their senses and escape from the trap of the devil, who has taken them captive to do his will.

2 Timothy 2:25-26

..."It is not the healthy who need a doctor, but the sick. I have not come to call the righteous, but sinners."

Mark 2:17

Often the enemy hits the stander with anger, bitterness, doubt, unbelief, jealousy, weariness and loneliness. How long should anyone wait for their spouse to come home? How long does the Lord wait for us to come home to Him? He often waits a lifetime for many of His children to come home. On their death bed of pain and suffering, at the end of their life, they cry out to a God that they rejected for possibly 60, 70 or 80 years!! Oh, that you would have that unconditional love, compassion and mercy for your loved one and family members!

Yes, you may have to die to your selfish desires of having a spouse meet your daily needs, but your Lord can meet them instead. A stander who had a answer to prayer for her finances wrote us to share her victory and signed off with "Jesus is a good husband." Did you marry for a lifetime or only for a season? When you said your marriage vows did you mean them, "For better or worse, richer or poorer, in sickness and in health?" I can say that in our marriage we have experienced each of these areas. We have a covenant marriage with our Lord. I praise the Lord regularly that He gave me a second, third and fourth chance when I was being disobedient during our marriage separation. I was so mad and angry at Bob and at God for allowing Bob to treat me so badly. I have to admit I was mad at God when He did not just "zap" Bob out of his sinfulness or that He did not punish him for his sins! Have you ever thought those thoughts? If you have, just stop and repent to your Lord. He understands and He stills loves you.

A few months later we received another letter from a stander who had chosen not to wait any longer for their spouse to come home. I asked the Lord the question, "Why?" Since He often speaks to me through His Word, I opened my Bible and the scripture below leaped off the page:

...for they did not believe in God or trust in his deliverance.
Psalm 78:22

I pray today that you will again go to your Lord and ask His will for your life. Yes, it is going to be a sacrifice. Your Lord shed His blood for you and for your family. Often something that is very valuable is very expensive. There is a price for you to pay for your spouse and loved ones **NOT** to go to Hell.

Mothers and Fathers, God is asking you to stand in the gap for restoration of your marriage so that you will NOT pass on separation and divorce for generations to come. May you pass on to your children the heritage and legacy of being a powerful prayer warrior, a man or woman of God, an intercessor for your nation, a man or woman of faith believing in miracles for God to heal bodies from diseases as well as marriages.

I pray that you will consider the price that Jesus paid for your salvation and surrender your life to being bold and standing against divorce. Pray for each marriage to be touched by your Lord Jesus Christ.

... *"With man this is impossible, but not with God; all things are possible with God."*

Mark 10:27

Always remember that even though the enemy has tried to destroy your marriage, *"no weapon forged against you will prosper."* **No weapon means none. Now you need to believe in your Lord God.**

...*Those who wage war against you will be as nothing at all. For I am the Lord, your God, who takes hold of your right hand and says to you, Do not fear; I will help you.*

Isaiah 41:12-13

Don't ever give up!

LEARNING TO WALK

For you were once darkness, but now you are light in the Lord. Walk as children of light (for the fruit of the Spirit is in all goodness, righteousness and truth), finding out what is acceptable to the Lord.

Ephesians 5:8-9 NKJV

What simple verses, but so hard to live at times, especially when enduring marriage and family problems at home. God calls you and me to be "stepping in the light" today and every day. The first step in your *Spiritual Journey* toward a healed family is to learn to walk.

Did you ever stop to consider that you might be the only glimpse of your Lord Jesus that some people ever see? They do not go to church, but they notice the logo on the back of our cars, or the Bible on the desk, but never see it being opened. Even the postman notices what kind of mail you receive. Does it match up with that Christian logo by the front door? When you eat out, the server observes you praying, and then you leave a minimal tip. Will that person see a stingy Jesus? My Lord is not! Those closest to you overhear a phone call about you standing with God and then in the next call they hear you rip someone apart. Is that like Jesus?

In the verses above, God's Word calls you to be consistent, yet do you live as if there were no God? Do you make a mockery of sin by your life? May today be the day your walk matches your talk.

In **Ephesians, chapter 5**, we are taught how to walk:

See that you walk circumspectly, not as fools, but as wise.
(Verse 15 -Walk Uncompromising)

redeeming the time, because the days are evil.
   (Verse 16 - Walk Urgent)
Therefore do not be unwise, but understand what the will of the Lord is.
   (Verse 17 - Walk Understanding)   **NKJV**

We have five grandchildren. When they were babies they kept growing every month. Before they were a year old each of them took their first few clumsy steps. Once that happened, it was not long before they were all running and playing with their siblings and cousins. None of them will ever want to go back to crawling again.

If you have not been walking the Christian walk in total obedience, may today be the day that you take the first few stumbling steps. It will not be long until you are running the race that the Bible describes.

OUR GOD CAN FIX ANYTHING!

"I am the Lord, the God of all mankind. Is anything too hard for me?"

Jeremiah 32:27

Do you believe that God can do anything? Do you believe God can take the impossible and fix it? Do you really believe God can restore and rebuild your marriage? Is anything too hard for God?

Today working full time at the Ministry office, Bob, Lori, our daughter and I mailed out our monthly tapes. I just praise the Lord that Bob and I are able to serve the Lord full time and totally dedicate our lives to having a part with Him in restoring marriages.

While packing the tapes, we played a video tape from Pastor David Wilkerson. of Times Square Church, titled *"Our God Can Fix Anything."* It was such a powerful sermon!

Do you really believe that God can fix anything? That was David Wilkerson's question. May I ask you to search your heart also. The answer is GOD IS ABLE! The problem is that you MUST believe. You need to get rid of your doubt and unbelief. You must want whatever to be fixed and get rid of your deadlines! Ask yourself, "Have I given up already in my heart?" Keep on believing!

Start believing in the power and awesomeness of your God. How big is your God? Our God can do anything! Now start; **Obey Him, Believe Him and Trust Him.**

Jesus replied, "What is impossible with men is possible with God."

Luke 18:27

Throughout the sermon, Pastor Wilkerson kept talking about marriages, prodigals, finances, and other trials. He said we should never give up on a marriage! Pastor Wilkerson is now praying for other men of God who are leaving the ministry and getting divorced. He is not giving up on the sinners! PTL!

"I know that you can do all things; no plan of yours can be thwarted."

Job 42:2

"Listen and hear my voice; pay attention and hear what I say...His God instructs him and teaches him the right way....All this also comes from the Lord Almighty, wonderful in counsel and magnificent in wisdom."

Isaiah 28:23,26,29

Someone may say your marriage is hopeless--remember what Jesus would say: **"NO ONE IS HOPELESS!!"**

BE AN EXAMPLE!

"May the words of my mouth and the meditation of my heart be pleasing in your sight, O Lord, my Rock and my Redeemer."

Psalm 19:14

Allow the Holy Spirit to use your words to proclaim the stand you are taking. We are often asked, "Should I tell my spouse what I am doing?" I told Bob many times that I was praying for him to come home. I also told him that I had made a huge mistake by divorcing him, and asked for his forgiveness. I had given up on God and on Bob.

During that conversation, I told him I had made a covenant and a vow and would wait forever for him to come back home. I shared what the Lord had revealed to me and that I was willing to wait even if he had to marry someone else and then end up in another divorce.

The Lord gave me many different scriptures during that special time in my life. I talked and walked in faith. I wore my wedding rings and told Bob I would keep them on for life, waiting for him. That also helped keep temptation from me. If men saw me, it spoke and showed others, "I am not available."

I recall that after we divorced, I took down all our family pictures with Bob in them. When I repented and totally surrendered my life to my Lord, those same family pictures went back up. Why? I wanted to proclaim to everyone that came into our home that I was loving Bob unconditionally. My marriage was dead, but I believed that the Lord was going to bring it back to life.

"'This is what the Sovereign Lord says: On the day I cleanse you from all your sins, I will resettle your towns, and the

ruins will be rebuilt.'"

Ezekiel 36:33

"'...I will put breath in you, and you will come to life. Then you will know that I am the Lord.'"

Ezekiel 37:6

Do not worry what your spouse or loved ones will say about you. Only care what your Lord God thinks and knows about you. Use our Lord as an example. You are walking in faith. You are becoming and acting as an Abraham or a Sarah. **(Read Hebrews 11:8-12)**

To this you were called, because Christ suffered for you, leaving you an example, that you should follow in his steps. "He committed no sin, and no deceit was found in his mouth." When they hurled insults at him, he did not retaliate; when he suffered, he made no threats. Instead, he entrusted himself to him who judges justly.

I Peter 2:21-23

Examine yourself and make changes where needed so that your stand may be a godly example to your spouse, your friends, your family, your pastor, and to other couples facing problems. *Lord, make me your soldier in this spiritual battle. Let me stand tall and shine so that You receive the praise. Amen.*

ARE YOU PERSECUTED?
YOU ARE BLESSED!

"Blessed are those who are persecuted because of righteousness, for theirs is the kingdom of heaven. Blessed are you when people insult you, persecute you and falsely say all kinds of evil against you because of me. Rejoice and be glad, because great is your reward in heaven, for in the same way they persecuted the prophets who were before you."
Matthew 5:10-12

Please memorize the above scripture. I pray that it will instantly come to your mind when someone comes against you because you are living for the Lord. If you are going through difficult times right now, may this scripture remind you that you are blessed when people come against you. When you choose to be different, you may be criticized or ridiculed. God's standards are not always popular or accepted as normal.

"But I tell you: Love your enemies and pray for those who persecute you, that you may be sons of your Father in heaven...Be perfect, therefore, as your heavenly Father is perfect."
Matthew 5:44,48

Seek to uphold God's standards of truth, justice and purity refusing to compromise with the present society of lukewarm believers. The enemy will tempt you to compromise God's will in order to avoid shame, embarrassment or loss. If the Lord has led you to stand for your marriage, do what He is calling you to do! Only when you get to heaven will you truly understand God's will and plan for your entire life.

"If you belonged to the world, it would love you as its own. As it is, you do not belong to the world, but I have chosen you

out of the world. That is why the world hates you."
John 15:19

Ask the Lord to give you love and forgiveness for your enemies, even when they are trying to hurt and destroy your family. Remember what Jesus said on the cross:

"Father, forgive them, for they know not what they are doing."
Luke 23:34

Read **Luke 6:27-36.** May you strive to be more like Jesus every day, applying His principles and precepts to your daily life. Your Lord will bless you for your obedience and faithfulness.

"Do to others as you would have them do to you."
Luke 6:31

LET'S MEASURE YOUR LOVE TODAY

"I love you," can be said very easily. Each stander around the world would be given a miracle if their spouse would say, "I love you and I want to come home." Instead, there are thousands of brokenhearted, wounded and rejected spouses today. You can point fingers at many people, but as YOU continue on your *Spiritual Journey,* measure your love today by reading **Romans 12:9-21**.

Some of the scriptures are:

"Love must be sincere....Be joyful in hope, patient in affliction, faithful in prayer....Bless those who persecute you; bless and do not curse....Do not repay anyone evil for evil....Do not take revenge, my friends, but leave room for God's wrath, for it is written: "It is mine to avenge; I will repay," says the Lord....Do not be overcome by evil, but overcome evil with good."
Romans 12:9-21 *(excerpts)*

How would you measure your love toward your spouse today? May you NOT allow the anger, bitterness, jealousy, fits of rage and unforgiveness ruin your heart. It will destroy you and any hope for restoration of your marriage. When your spouse sees or talks to you, what do they see? What do they sense by your body motion? Will they see unconditional love--love that is truly sincere?

Do not allow the enemy to steal from you any longer!

If I have the gift of prophecy and can fathom all mysteries and all knowledge, and if I have a faith that can move mountains, but have not love, I am nothing.
I Corinthians 13:2

I did not understand what love was until after my

divorce. One of the scriptures that the Lord gave me early in my standing and praying for Bob was **I Corinthians 13:4-8.** I used to pray both Bob and my name in it daily. I found out that I did not show the unconditional love of the Bible to Bob before we were divorced. The Lord showed me I had kept a record of wrongs and held grudges. The Lord taught me that I had to walk in unconditional love regardless of Bob's behavior. I was only responsible for my own behavior. I had a choice to treat him with "tough love" or love him as Jesus would.

Love is patient, love is kind. It does not envy, it does not boast, it is not proud. It is not rude, it is not self-seeking, it is not easily angered, it keeps no record of wrongs. Love does not delight in evil but rejoices with the truth. It always protects, always trusts, always hopes, always perseveres. Love never fails.

I Corinthians 13:4-8

"And now these three remain: faith, hope and love. But the greatest of these is love."

I Corinthians 13:13

You are crying out to the Lord to increase your faith and to increase your hope, but cry out now to INCREASE YOUR LOVE for your spouse. Because of what your prodigal spouse is doing, the enemy is using your emotions and feelings to cover up and even destroy your love for your spouse. May you be sensitive to the enemy's tricks.

"Do everything in love."

I Corinthians 16:14

A PRAYER FOR YOU

Lord, today You have many hurting, wounded and rejected children around the World. Would You go to each home and put Your loving arms around them and say, "I love you. I know how you hurt." The Lord wants you to "Trust Him and He will turn this around to good for you and your family. Hold on. Be still and know that I am God. I created the heavens and the earth and nothing is too hard for Me. Just believe and trust Me."

Thank You Lord, that You love all our spouses more than we do and You want all our marriages restored on the solid rock of Jesus Christ. Lord we ask You to have the Holy Spirit pour unconditional love into each of us so that we know it is a different kind of love and we will give You the praise for all that You do. In Jesus name we pray. *Amen.*

Have a blessed day because you are loved.

LET'S PRAISE THE LORD

"Sing to the Lord, for he has done glorious things; let this be known to all the world."

Isaiah 12:5

Sing to the Lord a new song; sing to the Lord, all the earth. Sing to the Lord, praise his name; proclaim his salvation day after day. Declare his glory among the nations, his marvelous deeds among all peoples. For great is the Lord and most worthy of praise; he is to be feared above all gods.

Psalm 96: 1-4

How are you doing on your *Spiritual Journey*? Let's praise the Lord today, regardless of your circumstances. Our Lord created you to worship and praise His Holy Name. Put aside all your trials and tribulations and think about God's awesome power as Creator of the universe. As the Creator of the Heavens and the earth, you need to learn to trust His power in your daily life. You have to learn to surrender every moment of your life to His will and His way.

Let us pray in agreement that our Nation will come to fear and reverence God. There are consequences to sin. Pray that our Nation will have a mighty revival, falling on their knees crying out to their Lord God.

Have you given up on God and on your spouse? I did. *But then* God touched and changed me when I thought our marriage was hopeless. I give all the praise to my Lord for all that He has done for Bob and me throughout our last seventeen years both personally and through this ministry.

"...Give thanks to the Lord, call on his name; make known among the nations what he has done, and proclaim that his name is exalted."

Isaiah 12:4

Spend time with the Lord basking in His mercy, grace and power. When you start to believe in the power of your Lord God, you can then walk in victory. You can *believe* and *expect* that your Lord will go after your lost prodigal. You know that your Lord loves your spouse and will deliver and save your loved ones from the bondages of sin. You must wait for His perfect timing.

As you praise your Lord, continue to pray interceding for your lost loved ones and our Nation, that you may continue to tell everyone around you the gospel of your Lord Jesus Christ.

...thanks be to God! He gives us the victory through our Lord Jesus Christ.
I Corinthians 15:57

May I remind you of Paul and Silas when they were stripped, beaten and severely flogged and then thrown into prison because of their faith. What was their reaction? They praised God, and look what happened.

About midnight Paul and Silas were praying and singing hymns to God, and the other prisoners were listening to them. Suddenly there was such a violet earthquake that the foundations of the prison were shaken. At once all the prison doors flew open, and everybody's chains came loose....The jailer called for lights, rushed in and fell trembling before Paul and Silas...."Sirs, what must I do to be saved?" They replied, "Believe in the Lord Jesus, and you will be saved--you and your household."
Acts 16:25-26,29-31

I pray that you will continue to pray for ALL prodigal spouses will repent and be saved. There is power in praying and praising the Lord. Praise defeats the enemy. When you get discouraged, read the Psalms and praise the Lord!

COUNT YOUR BLESSINGS!

Do you have a hymnal in your home? We have several. Bob and I are old enough that we still like hymns. It is also very interesting to read the stories how the hymns were written. Do you recognize the hymn *Count Your Blessings?* The words are excellent:

(CHORUS):
Count your blessings, name them one by one;
Count your blessings, see what God hath done;

1) When upon life's billows you are tempest tossed, When you are discouraged, thinking all is lost, Count your many blessings, name them one by one, And it will surprise you what the Lord hath done.

2) Are you ever burdened with a load of care? Does the cross seem heavy you are called to bear? Count your many blessings, ev'ry doubt will fly, And you will be singing as the days go by.

3) When you look at others with their lands and gold, Think that Christ has promised you his wealth untold; Count your many blessings, money cannot buy, Your reward in heaven, nor your home on high.

4) So, amid the conflict, whether great or small, Do not be discouraged, God is over all; Count your many blessings, angels will attend, Help and comfort give you to your journey's end.

(Hymn-Public Domain)

I hope the chorus and verses are running through your mind. Why? Because I would like you to start journaling, counting the many blessings you may often forget that you receive. Many of you forget answers to prayers, unless you write down your earnest prayer requests. I pray that you have already started a diary or a *Spiritual Journey* journal, where your thoughts, your emotions, your fears, and answered prayers can be written down as you study and read the Word. As you pray, if the Lord brings to mind thoughts, something or someone to pray for, write it down. If the Lord gives you a special scripture, a dream, a vision, a blessing--write it down and date it, so you will never forget that your Lord God is with you every moment directing your every step. We need to count our blessings even in the darkest of storms.

"...Lord, save us! ....He replied, "You of little faith, why are you so afraid?" Then he got up and rebuked the winds and the waves, and it was completely calm.
Matthew 8:25-26

Your Lord wants you to know that He loves you so very much. He is with you and He will calm your storm. Trust Him. Thank God for the Disciples who wrote about our Lord. May this encourage you to write about your spiritual walk, so that you can share with your children and grandchildren, what the Lord has done for you and your spouse. In doing so, you will teach them how to face their own trials should they come up in their lives.

If you fully obey the Lord your God and carefully follow all his commands I give you today, the Lord your God will set you high above all the nations on earth. All these blessings will come upon you and accompany you if you obey the Lord your God.
Deuteronomy 28:1-2

Why not start a list of all the blessings that you have right now? Remember, that your receive blessings by being obedient in your walk with the Lord. You will be surprised at what He has already done for you!

A BOBSERVATION

My greatest blessing? A praying, standing wife, who would not give up on me when everyone thought she was "crazy, had grounds to divorce me, was not adjusting, needed to get on with her life," and all the rest of the stuff that you are hearing every day.

During her crisis, Charlyne learned to pray (and to journal). Her prayers not only brought me home to our family and to the Lord, but her prayers were heard by God, who raised me from hospital beds on two occasions. When the doctors said death was coming for me, Charlyne claimed that Jesus was coming as the Great Physician, and indeed He did!

Your prodigal spouse needs a spouse who can pray, today and for the rest of your lives. A journal will give praise to the Lord in days ahead.

DO WE SEE RESTORED MARRIAGES?

Yes, Indeed we do! Bob and I have ten to twelve inches of restored marriages in notebooks! I bring the last week's praises to Rejoice Pompano Beach each Monday evening to share some of the restoration miracles.

We do not publish many of these for two reasons. Foremost, the returned prodigal needs to be in a spiritual incubator for a period of time after returning home. We have discovered that it takes about eighteen months before the prodigal is "over it" and be able to share what had happened. We both pray that you will allow your spouse to heal before sharing details with others. (No, your marriage will not be different. The timing needs to be that of the Lord.)

The second reason that we do not publish every restored marriage story is so that God, and not Rejoice Marriage Ministries, receives the glory. We appreciate the kind words people share, but it would be self-serving for us to publish boasting about this ministry. It is the Holy Spirit, and not a ministry nor a book, that restores marriages.

With that said, we do want to share a restoration email we received. It comes from a friend and is reprinted with her consent:

"Your ministry was the first thing I found the night I prayed for guidance on what the Lord wanted me to do in marriage. I was separated 16 months from a 23 year marriage. Your e-mail encouraged me so much through this journey. I know that the Lord will bless you abundantly for your unconditional love to his families. My husband is home. Yes, Bob, he is wounded but praise God, He will finish what He started. Every day God is giving me miracles through my husband. He also came home physically needing help. I consider it an honor to be there for him. You sent me your book on God does heal hurting marriages and hurting bodies. What a BLESSING!!! I know the Lord will restore his health totally!!!

"PRAISE GOD MY MIRACLE CAME HOME!!! In fact I told my husband that today!!! The day before he came home he said, 'You do realize that I am coming home with nothing, do you understand that?'

"I said 'Probably more than you may think I do.' One day he will read and hear the tapes of what I had learned while he was gone. Right now I am not asking questions just listening. It is an honor to wait on him and care for him."

HEALED!

"I will heal their waywardness and love them freely, for my anger has turned away from them."

Hosea 14:4

We received an email from a stander, "Praise the Lord! The Lord has restored our marriage! I am overwhelmed by all that He is doing in our lives!"

Another marriage was touched by our Lord Jesus Christ! I looked up the dictionary meaning of HEALING: is to make sound, well, or healthy again, restore to health, to cure or get rid of, to free from grief, troubles, evil, to reconcile.

"If my people, who are called by my name, will humble themselves and pray and seek my face and turn from their wicked ways, then will I hear from heaven and will forgive their sin and will heal their land."

2 Chronicles 7:14

Our Lord God is waiting for His children to repent and turn from their sins. God is a loving and just God. Our world is living as if there is no consequence to sins. There are consequences to sinfulness.

"When you spread out your hands in prayer I will hide my eyes from you; even if you offer many prayers, I will not listen. Your hands are full of blood; wash and make yourselves clean. Take your evil deeds out of my sight! Stop doing wrong, learn to do right! Seek justice, encourage the oppressed. Defend the cause of the fatherless, plead the case of the widow. "Come now, let us reason together," says the Lord. "Though your sins are like scarlet, they shall be as while as snow; though they are red as crimson, they shall be like wool. If you are willing and obedient, you will eat the best from the land; but if you resist and rebel, you will be

devoured by the sword." For the mouth of the Lord has spoken."

Isaiah 1: 15-20

Be encouraged that God does speak to prodigals and to His children. Pray for your spouse to be obedient and willing to follow the Lord's leading. Pray that you will be obedient and willing to make the changes that the Lord is asking you to make today.

May you be burdened about all the prodigals who are not home with their families. Let's pray and agree together that on each Sunday there will be a mighty harvest worldwide because God' s people prayed in unity and agreement. Bind the enemy and put a hedge of thornbushes around all the prodigals, so that they may come to their senses, **SUDDENLY!**

Our Heavenly Father is a Deliverer, a Restorer, and a Healer. Allow Him to deliver, restore and heal your spouse and your marriage. You just need to believe in His mighty power. Praise and thank Him daily for all that He is doing in your spouse's life that you cannot see.

"At that time I will gather you; at that time I will bring you home. I will give you honor and praise among all the peoples of the earth when I restore your fortunes before your very eyes," says the Lord."

Zephaniah 3:20

Praise the Lord for His faithfulness!

WAS IT WORTH IT?

Dennis Wingfield is our Board member and friend who writes a weekly *Standing Firm* email newsletter for men. I want to share portions of one of Dennis's newsletters with you because it is so powerful! Bob, Dennis, and I are very concerned that some of you do not understand the REASON that the Lord is asking for you to stand in the gap for your loved one. You may not understand that the Lord loves your spouse enough to not give up on them regardless of what they are doing now. May Dennis's comments and other scriptures encourage you as you continue on your *Spiritual Journey*.

Dennis wrote:

"I received an e-mail this week asking how I felt about standing for my marriage, having it restored, only to have my wife taken away into the Lord's arms. I stood straight up in my chair, pondering the significance of this question. I was being asked to weigh the return relative to the investment, as if standing was a financial transaction. Never in the ten years of standing for the healing of my marriage did I ever consider the cost to me personally for having my wife come home first to the Lord, then to me.

"Getting back to the original question, "Was it worth it?" Of course it was! By sacrificing my life, my precious wife, Therese, gained eternal salvation. I am humbled that the Lord used me in this way. Who am I to be so blessed by the Lord? I am joyful that Therese is home with the Lord. I can think of no greater gift than eternal salvation for a loved one.

"Marriage is *NOT* about getting one's own needs met. It has everything to do with meeting the needs of your spouse."

Be imitators of God, therefore, as dearly loved children and

live a life of love, just as Christ loved us and gave himself up for us as a fragrant offering and sacrifice to God.
Ephesians 5:1-2

"Jesus is our role model of self-sacrificial love. To "live a life of love," we need to do continuous acts of kindness for the betterment of our spouses. Love is "other" focused. Love does not focus on getting one's own needs met.

Wives, submit to your husbands as to the Lord....Now as the church submits to Christ, so also wives should submit to their husbands in everything.
Ephesians 5:22,24

Husbands, love your wives, just as Christ loved the church and gave himself up for her to make her holy, cleansing her by the washing with water through the word, and to present her to himself as a radiant church, without stain or wrinkle or any other blemish, but holy and blameless.
Ephesians 5:25-27

"Through Christ's sacrifice on the cross, His church is "holy and blameless." We husbands are called to love our wives with the same sacrificial love. By praying scripture for a prodigal spouse, you are cleansing her by the washing with water through the word...to present her to himself...without strain or wrinkle or any other blemish, but holy and blameless." Can you not see the important task at hand? We have the responsibility to God and our wives to pray for them, sacrificing our own needs, so that they may become holy!

"Christ did not consider the cost of sacrificing His life for the saving of many souls. We as spouses also, should not consider the cost of standing for the salvation of our mates. How can you put a price on a spouse's eternal salvation? Your goal in standing should not be the healing of your marriage, but that your spouse comes back to the Lord. Until your spouse is reconciled to God, he/she can never be reconciled to you. So many today exclaim, "What about my needs?" Marriages would not be in the trouble they are in today if we stopped thinking about ourselves and started thinking about meeting the needs of our spouses.

"We are not our own. Everything we are or have belongs to the Lord. We honor God when we sacrifice our own needs to meet the needs of our spouses."

Dennis is a special friend. He has written his first book, *Standing For God's Best.* May I share Dennis's words from his epilog from his book:

"Why have I told you all this? I want to stress the importance of the stand you are taking for the salvation of your family. What would have become of my wife if she did not have a one-flesh husband standing and praying for her? Where would my wife be spending eternity if I had "gotten on with my life" as the world so strongly suggests? We are fighting a spiritual battle for the souls of our loved ones! This is not about meeting our own selfish needs of companionship. This is about our prodigal spouses coming home to the Lord! It is about their eternal salvation!"

Bob, Dennis and I want to say to you that it is worth the price. *Never give up on your spouse!* It is only by God's grace and mercy that it is not each one of us being the prodigal!

BE IN LABOR!!

I have been talking to several people who are getting ready to go into labor to birth their miracle. They are prepared to have their "miracle baby" soon. They have been pregnant for a long time and now is the time to go into labor to birth their "miracle." God is moving.

Bob and I wish we could share all the news we are hearing. There was a wedding recently for a couple who had been divorced for 5 years. They had their anniversary recently without anything happening, but suddenly afterwards he has come home!!

Prodigals are calling and talking to standers that they have not seen or heard from for weeks, months or years. Prodigals are coming around more often to our stander's home and staying around with the family. PTL! The prodigals are testing the waters to see if there is any way that they could come back home and live! Love your spouse unconditionally and allow the prodigal to sense the Holy Spirit in your home.

Let us fast and pray for all our prodigals around the whole world.

Are you hurting and in pain today? Then maybe you are in the pains of childbirth. You are in labor. Let's travail for your spouse and your family. What do I mean?

My dear children, for whom I am again in the pains of childbirth until Christ is formed in you, how I wish I could be with you now and change my tone, because I am perplexed about you!

Galatians 4:19

What does the Webster's Dictionary say about labor?

"Physical, or mental exertion; work; toil; or to undergo, and suffer the pains of childbirth;"

Travail mans: *Very hard work; toil, labor pains; pains of childbirth; intense pain; agony, involving painful effort.*

"A woman giving birth to a child has pain because her time has come; but when her baby is born she forgets the anguish because of her joy that a child is born into the world. So with you: Now is your time of grief, but I will see you again and you will rejoice, and no one will take away your joy."
John 16:21-22

A stander who is a nurse in Minnesota wrote a thought that we are going to share with you about standing and the pains that each of you have at different times compared to being "pregnant". Let's compare having a baby with being in labor for our "miracle:"

"Many of us have heard the expression "praying through," but I want to give you another thought - this is about "pushing through." As a nurse, I spent many years in the hospitals assisting women in labor. When the end of the labor came, when it was time to push the baby out, if the mother did not push through the pain, if she did not cooperate with the process her body was going through, it would actually prolong the time to delivery. Of course, no woman really "felt" like pushing, but it was my role as nurse and coach just to help her do it anyhow with each and every contraction. This would progress us toward the desired goal of delivery, feelings or no feelings.

"Perhaps some people may not know this, but the physical act of pushing a baby out is most effective during the pain of the contraction. This is because the voluntary work of the mother enhances the involuntary work of her uterus and the pushing becomes more effective. The Lord gives us physical examples with spiritual applications. Since I became so well acquainted with the labor process, He used that knowledge many times to show me how many of the same things are true regarding spiritual delivery. In this case, I believe He wants us to see how best to handle the pain of our present circumstances.

"We all know the many ways that we have chosen to handle that pain that have not been godly, including telling all to everyone. It has not helped. Furthermore the enemy wants us to believe that our pain or our circumstances will never go away. We know that is *not* the truth and we know that there is an answer and a better way if we listen to our 'labor coach', the Holy Spirit. He will tell us each move to make.

"In physical delivery, the mother sometimes feels she will never be delivered or that she cannot handle the pain, but the birth attendant has seen many deliveries and knows that with the mind set of taking one contraction at a time, the process will be over sooner than she thinks. The mother needs those of faith around her to support her at such a time, not those who would tell her of other unfortunate situations with poor outcomes.

"Surround yourself with a cloud of witnesses, witnesses to the power of God, and those who have faith to believe with you for God's will to come to pass in your family.

"We know all too well our painful times in our present circumstances. Here I would also like to say that much of what we consider painful may even be what the enemy wants to bring back to our minds to rethink and analyze. We cannot afford to do this. Our focal point needs to be our Lord and what He has said to us. If we come to our Father, praising Him, praying and claiming His promises during these most difficult times, we will see the quick results in the answers to our prayers. He will enable us to pray and claim His Word, standing in the gap for our loved ones. Would complaining or sharing all the details with others help to hasten the delivery? How much longer would it take a woman to deliver her baby if instead of pushing she wanted to tell everyone how badly she hurt with each contraction. Believe me, I have witnessed this-trying to reason with someone just to push and get it over with and all the woman wants to do is tell you how difficult it is. We called that "wasting the contraction."

In my own circumstances; "I have complained to others about every detail, but it never yielded the answer. Instead, I believe that the Lord wants us to see that it even delays the process. We serve a God who keeps His promises - He knows what He has spoken and He will bring it to pass. Going into the prayer closet, trusting Him in every situation that He has the way out, using the authority Jesus died to give us, and focusing on Him will give us the desire of our hearts.

"For those who are now sensing an urgency to see their captives delivered, let me encourage you to purpose to take your concerns to God alone, leave them with Him, walk in peace, and trust Him. At the same time we also are aggressively, consistently, persistently resisting the enemy, who has had our loved ones long enough! I believe that God wants to act speedily, suddenly, quickly. He is looking for those who will stand and even push through. Will you?"

Many patriarchs of our churches have birthed miracles and answers to prayers by travailing and laboring in the prayer closet. May we never do less than what our ancestors have done to receive victory for their prodigals who have gone astray!!

"In the same way, the Spirit helps us in our weakness. We do not know what we ought to pray for, but the Spirit himself intercedes for us with groans that words cannot express."
Romans 8:26

This is the confidence we have in approaching God: that if we ask anything according to his will, he hears us. And if we know that he hears us-whatever we ask--we know that we have what we asked of him.

I John 5:14-15

A PRAYER FOR YOUR SPOUSE
AND FAMILY

O Lord, I call to You; come quickly to me. Hear my voice when I call to You. You are our refuge and strength an ever-present help in trouble. Praise be to the Lord my Rock, who trains my hands for war, my fingers for battle. You are my loving God and my fortress, my stronghold and my deliverer, my shield, in whom I take refuge. Reach down Your hand from on high; deliver me, my spouse and my loved ones from the mighty waters. Answer me quickly, O Lord; my spirit fails. Let the morning bring me word of Your unfailing love, for I have put my trust in You. Show me the way I should go. Teach me, my spouse and my loved ones to do Your will, for You are my God; may Your good Spirit lead us on level ground. I pray that You will speak to my spouse in a vision of the night when deep sleep falls on them, as they slumber in their bed. Speak in their ears and terrify them with warning, to turn them from wrongdoing and keep them from pride. Thank You Lord, that You will give each of us a heart to know You, that You are our Lord. We will be Your people, and You will be our God, for we will return to You with all our heart. Lord, I believe in the name of the Son of God so that I may know that I have eternal life. This is the confidence I have in approaching You: that if I ask anything according to Your will, You hear me. And if I know that You hear me, whatever I ask--I know that I have what I asked of You. I praise You for Your acts of power, and I praise You for Your surpassing greatness. *Amen.*

(Taken from **Psalm 141:1, Psalm 144:1-2, 7, Psalm 143:7-8,10, Jeremiah 24:7, Job 33:15-17, I John 13-15, and Psalm 150:2**).

THE FINAL WORD

Keep praying! God is moving! Spouses are coming home! We are also hearing from many spouses who are having their prodigal call wanting to come home. Especially as your restoration time nears, the prodigal is constantly thinking, planning and scheming ways that they can break off their ungodly relationship. Some prodigals may start calling more or stop by more frequently. Love them unconditionally. Ask God to check your heart to be certain that you truly have forgiven your spouse for all that has happened. When they come home, do not bring up the past. Be like the prodigal Father in Luke 15:11-24. Welcome them home and PRAISE THE LORD!!

"But while he was still a long way off, his father saw him and was filled with compassion for him; he ran to his son, threw his arms around him and kissed him.

"The son said to him, "Father, I have sinned against heaven and against you. I am no longer worthy to be called your son.'

"But the father said to his servants, 'Quick! Bring the best robe and put it on him. Put a ring on his finger and sandals on his feet. Bring the fattened calf and kill it. Let's have a feast and celebrate. For this son of mine was dead and is alive again; he was lost and is found.'" So they began to celebrate.

Luke 15:21-24

There are have been so many spouses coming home that Bob and I wrote a book together, *After the Prodigal Returns/Standing After The Prodigal Returns.* Bob also taped a personal message to all prodigals called, *Prodigal to Prodigal.* These two resources will be very helpful in rebuilding and restoring your marriage.

Please pray that ALL prodigals will listen to the Holy Spirit, be obedient to the Holy Spirit, repent and run from their sinful lifestyle. They feel guilty and responsible for destroying another person's life. Most are afraid to tell the other person what they are concerned about and what will happen to them. Pray that the Lord works out all the details completely. Pray that all chains, blindness, deafness and soul ties be broken NOW in the name of Jesus! Let's continue to pray that "Thousands are coming back every week!" PTL!

God bless,
Charlyne Steinkamp

CHOOSE TO BELIEVE

A few months ago, at Monday night Bible study, my wife used the above phrase several times in her teaching. At one point, she said something poetic by accident, "You need to choose to believe. That's the only way you will be free." As often happens, she continued with part of her own testimony. It seemed almost as if she were giving each of the lines below in her teaching. The Lord started my wheels turning, and a few minutes later I shared these words with our group:

The thief came a knocking at my front door,
So I told my spouse there would be no more.
"You have the 'escape clause,'" many told me,
I expected after a divorce to be happy and free.

Something's wrong I thought, alone each night,
But why do I hurt when divorce seemed so right?
There is something amiss here when I hurt so,
My spouse sinned, but my tears they do flow.
Over and over the Lord God attempted to talk to me,
All I could do was worry about my mate being free.
Lord, I tried and failed doing it the world's way,
What, dear God, to me can you promise, do and say?

"Dear child, you can choose to believe My way today,
Divorce is not the answer, no matter what others say.
All the prodigal spouses around - no problem for Me,
For them, My son, Jesus, bled and died upon the tree."

"Today take a stand for your marriage to be made new,
With this being alone and hurting you can be through.
The path is not easy, I will lead all along the way,
After I, your God speaks to you, what can anyone say?

So now I am a stander, with Jesus as my best Friend,

Yes, Lord, yes, I choose to believe You to the end.
I believe that my spouse is on the way home tonight,
Enemy satan, evil one, you just lost another fight!
                                    - Robert E. Steinkamp

Friend, Charlyne and I pray that you will choose to believe as you make this *Spiritual Journey* toward a healed home. May your stand be strong, not because you have heard from the Steinkamps, but because you have heard from the Lord.

So do not throw away your confidence; it will be richly rewarded. You need to persevere so that when you have done the will of God, you will receive what he has promised.
                                    Hebrews 10:35-36

EPILOGUE

This book is going to print one year behind schedule. When Charlyne retired, one of her goals was to write another book. During Holy Week, 2001, as she was completing work on this project, Charlyne was unexpectedly diagnosed with life-threatening cardiac problems. Her heart was functioning at 15%.

Early Easter morning, three days later, I suffered a minor heart attack at home. During the following week, the manuscript for *Spiritual Journey* lay dormant, while my wife and I both underwent cardiac catheterizations at separate hospitals. My disease was found to be minor, to be controlled by medication. It was suggested that Charlyne be evaluated for a heart transplant.

Instead, she turned to the Great Physician, and to one human physician, who understood the value of prayer. During the past year, we have seen exercise, medication, rest, and prayer, increase Charlyne's heart function to near 60%.

I want you to know the words in this book have been written for you by a woman with a burden for sharing what God did for our family, and what He can do for your family as well. If my wife knew this to be her last day on this earth, she would be finding somewhere to proclaim this good news.

On behalf of your prodigal spouse, I thank you for taking this *Spiritual Journey* with my wife. May the Lord help you to grow into a person of prayer, one who is confident they can trust Him to overcome any roadblock the enemy attempts to put in the path of your precious family.

Bob Steinkamp

NOTES ON MY *SPIRITUAL JOURNEY*
TOWARD A HEALED MARRIAGE

"Have faith in God." Jesus answered. "I tell you the truth, if anyone says to this mountain, 'Go, throw yourself into the sea,' and does not doubt in his heart but believes that what he says will happen, it will be done for him."

Mark 11:22-23

NOTES ON MY *SPIRITUAL JOURNEY* TOWARD A HEALED MARRIAGE

"Have faith in God." Jesus answered. "I tell you the truth, if anyone says to this mountain, 'Go, throw yourself into the sea,' and does not doubt in his heart but believes that what he says will happen, it will be done for him."
Mark 11:22-23

NOTES ON MY *SPIRITUAL JOURNEY*
TOWARD A HEALED MARRIAGE

"Have faith in God." Jesus answered. "I tell you the truth, if anyone says to this mountain, 'Go, throw yourself into the sea,' and does not doubt in his heart but believes that what he says will happen, it will be done for him."
Mark 11:22-23

NOTES ON MY *SPIRITUAL JOURNEY* TOWARD A HEALED MARRIAGE

"Have faith in God." Jesus answered. "I tell you the truth, if anyone says to this mountain, 'Go, throw yourself into the sea,' and does not doubt in his heart but believes that what he says will happen, it will be done for him."
Mark 11:22-23

INTRODUCING

REJOICE MARRIAGE MINISTRIES

"SHARING GOOD NEWS
FOR HURTING MARRIAGES"

What Is The Problem?

ONE MAN AND ONE WOMAN FOR A LIFETIME is God's perfect plan for marriage given to us in the Bible. The divorce rate in the United States is close to 50 percent. Men and women who once stood at an altar before God and pledged to each other "for better, for worse, for richer, for poorer, in sickness and in health, to love and to cherish, *'till death do us part"* are leaving home to pursue selfish desires. They become prodigals, leaving behind brokenhearted children and wounded spouses. Many go on to other marriages, the large percentage of which also fail. Divorce is attacking families within the church. Satan is out to steal, kill, and destroy families and marriages.

What Is The Provision?

There is a solution to the divorce problem. Our Lord Jesus Christ can heal hurting marriages, **even when only one** of those involved turns to Christ, seeking marriage restoration. *REJOICE MINISTRIES* was born out of the needs of hurting couples. All across our nation are thousands of spouses who are standing and praying for God to restore their marriages. We invite you to allow us to stand and pray with you for the restoration of your marriage and home, regardless of the circumstances.

DO YOU REALLY

WANT A DIVORCE?

THERE IS HELP AVAILABLE

- Books and tapes to encourage you

- Bible study material to help you learn and grow in God's Word

- Daily email devotional from Charlyne

- Prayer partners to stand and agree with you in prayer

- Testimonies of others with restored marriages

"Be strong and courageous. Do not be afraid or terrified... for the Lord your God goes with you; he will never leave you nor forsake you." Deuteronomy 31:6

REJOICE MARRIAGE MINISTRIES

Bob and Charlyne Steinkamp
P.O. Box 10548
Pompano Beach, Florida 33061

(954) 941-6508
FAX (954) 781-7076

www.stopdivorce.org
www.rejoiceministries.org
www.rejoicenet.net

REJOICE MINISTRIES MATERIALS

BOOKS BY THE STEINKAMPS

* "Prodigals Do Come Home"
* "The Twelve Days of....?"
* "Thoughts On Restoring A Marriage"
* "After The Prodigal Returns/Standing After
    The Prodigal Returns"
* "More Thoughts On Restoring A Marriage"
* "Chicagoman"
* "Good News Online"
* "Charlyne Cares"
* "Be Healed"
* "A Day of Freedom"
* "Rejoice on the Road"
* "Days of Joy"
* "Pulpits in the Marketplace"
* "The Spiritual Journey Toward a Healed Marriage"
* "Rejoice on the Rails"

CHARLYNE CARES

Each day Charlyne Steinkamp sends out a daily email devotional to men and women around the world who are praying for their marriage. You can subscribe free by visiting **http://charlynecares.net**

REJOICE BIBLE STUDIES

Many of Charlyne's teachings at the Monday night Rejoice Bible study have been taped. Please contact us for an updated list of over one hundred tapes that are available. These have been recorded "live" so that you can experience the blessing of attending these sessions right from your home, or with other standers at one of several Rejoice Bible Studies meetings around the nation. Contact us for details.

THE GREATEST NEWS

"That if you confess with your mouth, ' Jesus is Lord,'
and believe in your heart that God raised him from the
dead, you will be saved." Romans 10:9

Many have found that the first step in a healed marriage is to have a personal relationship with Jesus Christ. Our God and Creator is waiting to hear your prayer. Have you received Jesus Christ as Lord and Savior of your life? He will save you and be your Comforter and Counselor in the days ahead, regardless of the circumstances.

A PRAYER FOR YOU

Dear Jesus, I believe that You died for me and that You rose again on the third day. I confess to You that I am a sinner and that I need Your love and forgiveness. Come into my life, forgive me for my sins, and give me eternal life. I confess to You now that You are my Savior and Lord. Thank You for my salvation. Lord, show me Your will and Your way for my marriage. Mold me and make me to be the spouse I need to be for my spouse. Thank You for rebuilding my marriage. **Amen.**

Signed_____

Date_____

..."Believe in the Lord Jesus, and you will be saved--
you and your household." Acts 16:31

YOUR RESPONSE

REJOICE MARRIAGE MINISTRIES
P.O. Box 10548
Pompano Beach, Florida 33061-7242

____Please add me to the newsletter mailing list.

____Please send information on marriage restoration.

____I want to help.

Enclosed is my donation of $ _____ (tax deductible)

(Please Print Clearly)

_____

NAME

_____

ADDRESS

_____

CITY, STATE, ZIP CODE

_____

PHONE   E-MAIL

_____

MY SPOUSE'S NAME

MY PRAYER REQUEST:_____

_____

_____